GONE FISHING
– Anecdotes of an Angler –

DENIS O'CALLAGHAN

VERITAS

Published 2008 by
Veritas Publications
7/8 Lower Abbey Street
Dublin 1
Ireland

Email publications@veritas.ie
Website www.veritas.ie

ISBN 978-1-84730-093-5

A catalogue record for this book is available from the British Library.

Designed by Lir Mac Cárthaigh
Printed in Ireland by Betaprint Ltd.

Veritas books are printed on paper made from the wood pulp of managed forests. For every tree felled, at least one tree is planted, thereby renewing natural resources.

Contents ✐

Introduction

Reading about fishing is part of the angler's world, particularly during the long dark days of the closed season. Your typical angler will have a selection of books on the art and science of catching fish. Older books will portray the human experience while distilling the knowledge and wisdom gained over the centuries. More modern ones tend to focus on the technical know-how, on the use of specialised tackle and lures which are the stock-in-trade of the professional angler, particularly those who enter serious competitions.

Personally, even though I have fished rivers and lakes for close on seventy years, these latter books do not attract me. They reflect an obsession with angling at its most basic level, the level of catching fish. In my young days that would have indeed fuelled my addiction, but then the primitive hunter-gatherer instinct mellowed into appreciation of the human experience, which fishing, either on my own or with a companion, has come to mean for me.

Those who observe from outside the circle of true initiates may judge that standing at the riverside or sitting in a boat by the hour looks like an exercise in gaining the virtue of patience through unrelieved boredom. They may see it as the Western equivalent to what Indian Maharishis undertake to achieve the higher states of mystical detachment. If that observation were correct you would see very few anglers around. I cannot speak for the whole angling fraternity, so I will tell what angling has come to mean for me.

Let us first take the riverbank. It is a wonderland where you may leave the distractions of the world and become one with nature in all its moods and tenses. For that you must choose a promising location. If you do alright you will have the company of the varied forms of wildlife which have made their homes in and around the river. Anglers move slowly and carefully in plying their art and so their presence is readily accepted as part of the natural environment. They are not seen as a threat by wild creatures that are shy by nature. In the course of the book I will dwell on this at intervals.

Angling from a boat is quite a different experience. Its richness depends on the backdrop provided by the surrounding countryside. For me, words cannot describe the beauty of the terrain that embraces Lough Cloonaughlin. It is situated high in the Commeragh catchment system that feeds down to Lough Curane in Waterville. In bright sunshine it glows like a still painting etched by the hand of the Creator. It comes alive when shadows chase one another across the mountains. Close beside, by contrast, is Lough-na-Móna, for which one word will suffice – featureless. True enough, even in Cloonaughlin if you draw a blank at the fishing you can always pull ashore at a favoured spot. For such occasions, I will have to hand a book wrapped in plastic for a quiet read pending a change in the conditions. You then take up the rod with new zest.

Usually in boat angling one will have a companion or two. These will almost invariably have been lifelong friends who will share reminiscences of former times. We will relive those days again. As you later read the myriad stories about those choice characters, you will appreciate what colour they added to every hour we spent together.

'Think where man's glory most begins and ends/And say my glory was I had such friends' (W.B. Yeats, 'The Municipal Gallery Revisited'). I leave you with a question: why did Jesus choose four fishermen – Peter, Andrew, James and John – to rate as his special companions among the Twelve Apostles?

1. Getting Underway

Addiction to angling is a curious phenomenon. Many anglers still try to introduce their sons to the art but relatively few become converts and fewer still become addicts. One father told me that his son found the silence and lack of action not to his liking. There must be some preconditioning factor in the human psyche, a gene which stimulates those destined to make angling a lifelong commitment. Even though for me angling was always more of an experience beyond catching fish, I would surely qualify on those addictive terms. Early in our schooldays we had identified the possibilities offered by the little stream at the foot of Meelin village. We built dams to create pools on which to sail homemade boats. We constructed waterwheels to run complicated contraptions linking up a series of thread reels as pulleys. Where there was anything to do with water we were in our element. Anything to do with fish soon became the real focus of interest.

In the course of the preparatory works on the stream, we discovered that as we moved stones around tiny fish would dart from their hiding places. Jam jars were the very thing to capture them. My father identified these thumb-sized fish as gudgeons. They were lethargic, spending their days lying doggo on the bottom of the jar. We lost interest after the first inspection. It was a poor start to a lifelong interest. For most of my mates that ended any further exploration into the ways of fish. Not for me.

I had noticed that two neighbours, Bertie Cahill and Den Vaughan, would follow the line of our little stream down the glen with fishing rods on their shoulders. That was enough to fire the imagination. Decent men that they were, they made no objection to an inquisitive eight-year-old tagging along, particularly when they were allowed to do all the talking on everything connected with fishing, while I was an avid learner.

When we reached the Dallow river, all I had to do was keep out of the way and watch the action. Was I hooked? Was I what! I soon made myself useful by digging worms and catching minnows as bait. Indeed, I sought to make myself not just useful but indispensable, so that I would be welcomed as part of the team.

In those days a fishing rod was expensive. One needed to improvise. A straight length of hazel was serviceable enough for a beginner, and Den Vaughan did the necessary in fitting it out with the basic trappings and a spare reel. I was in business and never looked back.

That's how it all began. Those two friends on the banks of the Dallow live on in my memory. It seems just yesterday that they would follow their set routine on arrival at the river. Peering over the Black Bridge at Ballinatona, they would assess prospects based on the conditions of the flow and colour of the water. Was it porter coloured enough for the worm; beer tinted enough for the minnow; rippled and clear enough for the artificial fly; calm and sunny to suit the woodbee? I would respect their consensus on these important matters, knowing that they spoke from experience of local conditions.

I was an avid listener to all that hard-won wisdom. As a member of the team, I was made privy to the secrets of the trade. I learned early on that you do not show your hand when you meet up with other anglers on the river. The sense of competition prevailed. You might admit that a few fish were caught – but never never on which bait or fly you caught them. They wouldn't have believed you anyway! Of course, once you had returned to base later, with nothing much in the bag, it would be in order to varnish the truth. I recall one occasion when that backfired on a wily angler, who had told a rival that his most successful fly on the day was the Greenwell's Glory. As the rival bagged fish after fish my friend winked and whispered: 'You know what? It's time for a change to the Greenwell's Glory!' Anyone who is taken in by that universally accepted pattern of exaggeration by anglers has only himself to blame for his gullibility. There are lies, damn lies, statistics and fishermen's tales. Everyone is expected to be aware of that as a simple fact of life. It would be described in the moral text books as a broad mental reservation. One even wonders whether that report in the gospel story about the Apostles netting fifty-three huge fish at one throw of the net is a bit of an exaggeration. Maybe not so in that particular case under the all-seeing eye of the Risen Christ!

Anyway, at sundown, as the day's fishing on the Dallow drew to a close at the Black Bridge, there would be a detailed scrutiny of what went right and what went wrong. The protocol required that you never blamed the shortfall on your own incompetence or misjudgement. The conditions were just not right. Are they ever! Here an inventive mind should never be short of a reason, with all the elements offering so many ready excuses: 'Sure there will be other days anyway when the fish will prove cooperative'.

Memory brings back the walk home through the evening air scented by those roadside wildflowers: the meadowsweet and the woodbine. You kept in step with the rise and fall of the whirr of the jacksnipe, the *gabhairin rua*, in the darkening sky promising a fine day on the morrow. It was heaven on earth. I pray that Peter the fisherman welcomed those friends of yesteryear with an understanding nod when those white lies of ours may have registered as a footnote in the Book of Life. I pray that what will not be laid to their charge are the temptations they put in my way when angling displaced hours that otherwise would have been more profitably spent at the desk. In their defence, I plead that the enhanced quality time at work later more than balanced the equation.

By the way, there is nothing better to clear the mind of free-floating anxiety than a few hours with the fishing rod. The rod acts as a wand to exorcise the worries of the world. In terms of good sense for human survival, Jesus never said a truer word than in his advice about worry: 'Do not worry about tomorrow: tomorrow will take care of itself. Each day has enough trouble of its own'. A popular song takes up the theme: 'The cares of the morrow can wait until this day is done'. Once you hang out the shingle, 'Gone Fishing!' you throw the switch that locks care out of sight and out of mind. Bryan MacMahon, the Listowel writer, quotes the advice of an old schoolmaster: 'Let the sediment of the day settle in the well of the mind'. That sure is recreation at its most basic.

I appreciate that those on the outside will have little understanding of the spell cast by the fishing rod on otherwise quite normal people. In his oft-quoted definition of that same fishing rod, Dr Samuel Johnson described it in his dictionary as a stick with a worm at one end and a fool at the other. The man had no soul. Thank God for his contemporary Izaak Walton, author of *The Compleat Angler*, whose heart was in the right place. Looking back on a day's fishing over three centuries ago, he spoke for all of us: 'I'll tell you, scholar: when I sat last on this primrose bank, and looked down these meadows, I thought of them as Charles the Emperor did of the city of Florence: that they were too pleasant to be looked upon but on holy-days'. Isn't that a thought! I have often shared that feeling at sunset as I proclaim with the Psalmist: 'O Lord, our God how wonderful is your name over all the earth'. Is it any wonder that Izaak Walton subtitled his classic *The Contemplative Man's Recreation?* Spiritual writers of ancient times portrayed the beauty of nature as reflecting the splendour of the Almighty and singing a hymn to his glory. In that understanding we can correct that thought of Thomas Gray in his *Elegy Written in a Country Churchyard*:

Full many a gem of purest ray serene,
the dark unfathomed caves of ocean bear.
Full many a flower is born to blush unseen,
and waste its sweetness on the desert air.

Among all those alternative medicines in vogue today, nothing heals heart, mind and soul like a session with the fishing rod, ideally in company with another brother of the angle. Aromatherapy, hydrotherapy, lithotherapy, hypnotherapy, and whatever you are having yourself, may be advertised as antidotes to the free-floating anxiety which is endemic in our culture. Pride of place must still go to the natural curative powers of the fishing rod. True, a poor experience on the first day out may spell the end for a beginner. There is nothing predictable about fishing. Even the expert may have a blank day. Anyway, if you caught fish every time you cast a fly on water you would quickly lose interest.

I accept that many people are convinced that angling requires an intolerable level of patience. Patience, yes, but intolerable, no. An Irish proverb does stress that patience may have its place: *Éist le glór na habhann agus geóbhair breac.* If you listen to the song of the river you will sooner or later catch fish. There is always that promise in the sound of a running stream. To succeed you must persist in keeping that fishing line in the water. A dry line never caught a trout.

Another side of the patience factor is equally true – that is waiting for an angler to come off the water certainly needs patience! I recall an occasion when my companion on the river was expected home to celebrate his wedding anniversary. The fish were on the move and so was the clock as it ran well over the promised hour. On meeting up with him later that week, he described the frosty welcome from his wife: 'A picture but no sound'. I must thank my mother for waiting patiently in the car during many a journey when I came to an inviting stretch of stream. The good mother that she was, she would read my body language and suggest that I get out the fishing rod and she would later show – or feign – interest in the result.

One must admit that when conditions look promising we anglers are the most impatient and inconsiderate of people if anything thwarts our intent to get to the river. On one occasion I had undertaken to drive my mother to the hairdresser in Newmarket with a wedding in the offing. I had not realised how long the women's hairdressing operation takes. As time dragged on, with fishing conditions looking more and more promising for the evening, I came to steal a look inside the women's preserve to assess progress. She at once gave me my answer in a telling comment: 'Look at him now,' she said, 'and I waited nine months for him – and he cannot wait an hour or two for me!' Game, set and match to the lady under the hairdryer! I withdrew with as much dignity as I could muster.

Angling may seem a carefree sport but there are risks – particularly from cattle running free on riverside lands quite likely not to be fenced. Bulls can be a serious hazard in those circumstances. There is a story that in the early days of the Free State an inspector of bull licences stopped at a gate where a farmer was checking his livestock down in the riverside fields. The farmer questioned the third party's right to go on his land, but the inspector produced his credentials and vaulted the gate. Whatever about the farmer's reservations, the young cross-bred bull, then called a Sinn Féiner, indicated serious exception to this intrusion on his territory. The inspector took to his heels shouting to the farmer for help, 'Show him those papers of yours,' said the farmer, 'and sure you'll be ok!'

I never had a call as close as that, but I had a few scares, particularly from a treacherous animal, which had open access to one of the best stretches of the Blackwater near Lombardstown. If the black Kerry bull is notorious for deadly cunning, the young Friesian is not far behind in the rating. This animal of my acquaintance would not give a warning bellow. He would stalk you with stealth and with malice aforethought and then announce his arrival with a snort. At that late warning, direct evasive action was of the essence. This once left me up to my waist in a pool while he threw up earth along the bank. Having taught me a lesson, he ambled off, lowing hoarsely back to the grazing herd. On further expeditions after that sobering experience, one would continuously check his location and keep a safe distance.

We have all heard how some item that bodes no good is described as 'showing a red rag to a bull'. True or not, we anglers certainly believe it and typically wear sober-coloured gear. Anyway, flashing anything bright or colourful does not help the fishing. Some people will dismiss that proverb about a red rag challenging the bull with the claim that the animal is colour-blind. The matador in the bull ring knows better. When he wants the animal to focus on him he flutters that red veil. True enough, it may just be part of the drama in the ring. Better not take any chances on the riverbank.

A bull running free with a bunch of heifers is at his most dangerous in August and September, the natural season for cows to be in heat. One might think that in themselves heifers do not constitute a risk, but that is where you make a big mistake. Nothing is more dangerous than cattle on the loose with suckling calves. Every angler knows it. A heifer's protective maternal instinct is very strong, particularly when anything threatening or unusual comes into sight. In the old days they were accustomed to having people familiarly around – unlike today when part-time farmers are now more the rule and may be seen as strangers.

A suckling herd is particularly averse to dogs, especially large dogs. I had one such bad experience with Deise, an old red setter. A single nervous heifer gave a warning bellow which said 'Danger!' The herd charged, pinning the dog to the base of a ditch. Canny old warrior that he was he glued his body into the angle of the fence, as the animals in turn tried in vain to gore him. They were berserk. I would equally be at risk if I intervened. I worked around from behind the fence and crawled up on the bank. I reached down during a lull and yanked him to safety. After that he gave all cattle a wide berth.

In spite of what I have said about danger from outside agencies, most emergencies on the river are self-inflicted.

Anglers survive into ripe old age by allowing a decent margin for error. One should never wade in running water unless absolutely necessary. Even when stepping carefully with waders, a fast-flowing current at the head of a pool can wash the gravel from under your feet. One must always keep in mind that river stone is round and typically slippery when coated with green algae. You never lift a leg, you shuffle. Keeping both feet on the ground is a good rule. This is more crucial in clear water where depth is deceiving and could hamper any effort to correct a stumble.

One false move and a mad scramble will see you washed into a pool with Wellingtons or waders pushing you under because of the trapped air inside them. Once I rescued a companion from that lethal predicament, as he steadied himself precariously with the staff of the net from being swept downstream by a strong current. The experience taught us both a hard lesson which brought home the truth of an Irish proverb: *Is fearr ciall ceannaighte ná dá ciall múinte.* On that count, one should always wear a lifejacket when fishing. The modern lifejacket is very tidy, little more than a vest. The secret is that it self-inflates when submerged in water. All anglers have been forewarned about the need to wear a lifejacket in a boat. Even on the riverbank it would have saved many a life.

Some of the more strident on the anti-blood sport side object to angling as a cruel exercise. This campaign is overkill and it tends to discredit their general cause. Personally, I have given up game shooting even though I still cherish my red setters, Deise and Cora. The house would not be a home without having them beside me. I continue to license the shotgun and will use it to control vermin such as the grey crows, which wreak havoc on young lambs and all ground-nesting birds. Any scruples you may have about disposing of grey crows evaporate when you witness the agony of lambs that have had their eyes plucked out. The thought of shooting an old warrior of a cock pheasant out of the sky in all his glory leaves me cold. Those reservations came to a head for me one January morning as the sun was burning off the hoar frost. An old monarch of a cock pheasant launched from under a holly tree, calling a challenge to the world now that the shooting season was almost over. Having raised the gun by conditioned reflex, I dropped it slowly to my side. That was that. Even the migratory woodcock, which is not territorial like the pheasant, is now left to enjoy life undisturbed by me. In these cases, once the question is raised there is just one answer.

Fish do not have individuality. Generally they are out of sight and lost in an anonymous shoal. One's emotions are not engaged. True, there are exceptions as all anglers know when they build a relationship with a particular fish, which stubbornly holds its station beside a rock in a favoured lie. Here I can appreciate the link with a very special fish, which Ernest Hemingway describes in *The Old Man and the Sea*. I have had the experience on more than one occasion. When an old stager lured by an artificial fly has made a mistake in a moment of carelessness, I slip him back safe into the water with advice to double-check next time. Strange enough, he may fall for a similar lure again when the humour takes him. In fact I caught one such fish carrying a hook and a length of cast from a previous encounter.

Now to get back to the ordinary run of fish. I do not have a scruple about taking them. Indeed, I question the logic of those who would ban angling as a sport. They may be out-and-out vegans or vegetarians, but does that entitle them to impose their personal preferences and moral opinions on others? Fish provide an important element of diet. For that the fish must be caught, generally by commercial methods. Does one accept that common practice and then reject the game angler? If so, the objection must attach to the sport factor rather than to the actual catching of the fish. It would be different if the angler took pleasure in cruelty, in the actual pain suffered by the fish.

The fisherman can certainly claim good scriptural warranty for his practice from gospel stories. Don't we constantly hear of the Apostles engaged in fishing? We do not have evidence that Jesus took direct part in the action, but as an accessory did he not instruct St Peter to procure a fish from the Jordan to pay the Temple tariff? Even though fish was never prescribed by the Church for days of abstinence, the impression was given that it was the standard substitute for meat. Indeed, the traditional calendar inscribed the sign of the fish as a reminder on those days. That sign also recalls the Greek term for fish, ICHTHUS used as an acronym of spelling out *Jesus Christ Son of God, Saviour*. This was the secret mark in days of persecution that identified Christians to each other.

Even though it does not focus attention specifically on fish, *The Catechism of the Catholic Church* shows good sense when it takes up the issue of mankind's role of stewardship in regard to animals: 'It is legitimate to use animals for food and clothing. They may be domesticated to help man in his work and leisure. Medical and scientific experimentation on animals, if it remains within reasonable limits, is a morally acceptable practice since it contributes to caring for or saving human life'. (par. 2417) *The Catechism of the Catholic Church* looks for balance when it states: 'It is contrary to human dignity to cause animals to suffer or die needlessly. It is likewise unworthy to spend money on them that should as a priority go to the relief of human misery. One can love animals; one should not direct to them the affection due only to persons'. (par. 2418) This is a sobering corrective to the extreme level of sentiment that drives people to lavish luxury on pets. A dog is at its best when it knows its place and is treated naturally as a dog.

All this makes good sense for fishing as well. Arbitrary cruelty is a horror. I would go further than the *Catechism* here. Being guilty of needless cruelty certainly offends human dignity but it is also surely wrong in itself. Literally in God's name, what could possibly justify it? The media frequently carry accounts of cats or dogs being thrown on to bonfires. Badger baiting and using rabbits to 'blood' hounds are only a step away, even though the actual infliction of pain is not the direct intent. The conscientious angler will be sensitive to allowing fish to suffer. A sharp tap on the back of the head delivers the *coup de grace*. This is the approved way of despatching a trout or salmon and to this purpose you would have the standard wooden baton stowed permanently in the boat. This was traditionally called the 'priest', evidently because it administered the last rites. One old fishing friend of mine, after a blank outing on the lake, would remark that the priest did not need to don the stole today.

⤙ 2. Down by the Riverside

In the process of angling we became familiar with everything that grew or lived on the riverbank and in the water. The size of a bag at the end of the day's fishing became incidental to the enjoyment of the total experience. There was such a variety of wildlife all around us. In the silence one would hear the corncrake rasping in the meadow and the cuckoo calling as it moved from tree to tree. The lonely cry of the curlew would forecast a change of weather for the worse on the morrow. Everything one saw or heard registered to build a sense of peace and contentment. Even in sad times nature falls in line with your mood. A familiar poem from our schooldays sees nature gently grieving with a mother who has lost a son:

Ag gabháil an sléibhe dom tráthnóna do labhair na héinlei-the liom go brónach. Do labhair an naosg binn 's an cro-tach glórach ag faisnéis dom gur eág mo stórach.

When I now take the red setters, Deise and Cora, for their evening run in the countryside around Mallow we are spoiled for choice. The favoured options are over Knockroura through the Coillte wood or along the Martin River at the back of the Stag on the old Grenagh-Blarney road. I know that if they could voice their vote they would opt for the riverbank. For them there is a greater variety of natural wildlife interest on the riverside than in the uniform Coillte plantation. The scent of pine is certainly invigorating but there is so little birdsong to lighten one's step. For me also, the riverside offers a fresh environment that changes with the seasons. Perhaps my vote for that is influenced by nostalgia for the past when I would have carried the fishing rod. The old Irish saying already quoted recalls that promise in the sound of running water, when that song of the river focuses the interest of any fisherman.

When I first took up the fishing rod in my home country, the limestone rivers Allow and Dallow were crystal clear. Unfortunately, there has been some deterioration over the years, but they still hold some trout fry. The minnow was an early casualty of pollution. These streams and their lesser tributaries were once excellent spawning grounds for Blackwater salmon. Naturally this attracted the attention of some locals, who would have been expert with gaff and torch. They did little damage to the overall stock because there was more than enough to spare. Anyway, the flesh of salmon on the spawning beds is of very poor quality and would not pass as edible today. Even in former times I think that the sense of adventure was what inspired the practice more than the end product. I am not sure whether the salmon still spawn in the upper regions and whether the fry survive in sufficient numbers for stock replacement. That depends on the water quality, because the solid limestone benches do not filter out the pollutants as shale would do.

This is where the Martin River should score. It draws its water through shale and sandstone, an excellent natural filtration medium. Were it not for that factor the pollutants from the surrounding catchment area would leech into the river in far larger amounts than at present. There have been some serious spillages everywhere from slurry holding tanks which have wiped out fish life over some distance down river of the spillage. Even though there would be recovery in time, a repeat incident would do major damage to new young stock.

To assess the health of the river, the sight of the water ousel, better known as the dipper, is good news indeed. It means that the bottom link of the food chain has recovered and there is hope for the fish – if they are given the time. The ousel is a good indicator of the quality of the water as the canary used to be of the quality of the air in the coal mines. Once the canary keeled over it was high time to evacuate the mine. The dipper is not quite the size of a rather plump blackbird, but it has a very distinctive white bib which you cannot miss as it bobs up and down on a stone just off the current. Now you see it – now it's gone! The bird has simply dipped out of sight down into the current where it locks on to pebbles with its claws and turns over stones searching for grubs and creepy-crawlies. Then it surfaces a few feet across the current. Follow that for an acrobat! They breed well on the Martin River near Blarney. You cannot miss the dipper's piercing whistle as it whirrs at great speed following every curve of the river just above the surface of the water.

You may be fortunate to spot another speedster along that same river. The kingfisher is as colourful as birds go – green/blue/orange. Usually all you see is that flash of colour and all you hear is a piercing cry as it disappears around the next bend. For such a lovely bird it is a very bad housekeeper. Outside the entrance to its nest in a hole in the riverbank or on the ledge to a bridge you will find refuse spread around. With the stench of fish bones the kingfisher could be fined for littering.

One bird that would have been very familiar back a generation or more in every stream, river and lake was the water hen. She was a silent mover as she clucked quietly, feeding along a weed bed. The flick of her white bob tail always caught the eye. One of the loveliest sights was the line of chicks in her wake as she sailed along among the weed beds. The tiny balls of black fur might seem helpless, but when she clucked an alarm they would skitter at speed for shelter. Alas, the water hen is close to extinction. You will not find them any more on the Martin River and few if any along the Navigation, cutting beside the Killarney road out of Mallow. This used to be a favourite haunt.

Suspicion falls on the mink. It is a voracious predator. A lone ranger, within a short time it will clean out every edible creature along its strictly territorial beat. The mink has no saving grace, neither in appearance nor behaviour. Everyone's hand is against it. It was a bad day that it made its way from breeders' cages into our native environment. Fortunately, it lacks intelligence. That stupidity is its downfall. It slips readily into a metre of four-inch plastic pipe, blocked at one end then set upright at a sharp angle and baited with a piece of fish. Once the mink slides inside there is no escape in reverse.

Henry Williamson's *Tarka the Otter* and Gavin Maxwell's *Ring of Bright Water* show the otter as intelligent, fun-loving and a good companion in or out of his house near the river. Everyone loves the otter with its cute face. Even anglers will not begrudge it the odd fish, taken all too often from the spawning bed. Its standard diet is the eel, which it noses out under stones and riverside debris. They are superb swimmers under water. What marks their progress is the trail of bubbles on the surface. Otters are playful animals and like tumbling into a pool as their kits learn to swim. They give the impression that they are happy to amuse an observer. Most normal people resent the practice of hunting them to death with a pack of otter hounds.

There is a variety of wildlife on every riverside, but you need to keep a sharp eye; most creatures do not advertise their presence. You cannot miss the awkward launch and screech of the heron as it scrambles into the air. In Ireland, the heron is commonly confused with the crane or the stork, which are not natives here. Herons are solitary birds, except at nesting time. If you ever come near a heronry you cannot miss the clacking of the beaks on the nests. The heron is the most awkward-looking bird in flight with trailing legs and slow wing flaps. In wading into position for a stab at a sprat with slow deliberate steps, it is most dainty and deadly. Allowing for the refraction in even a few inches of water it has an unerring aim. That beak strikes like an arrow. When my setter Cora ambushed one in the Martin River I feared for her eyes. I recalled how a friend had picked up a wounded heron. He rued the day. The bird struck him on the big toe through the Wellington and in a telling phrase 'put fire out his eyes'. So be warned.

One advantage of flora over fauna is that plants stay put. They do not disappear once you spot them, as wildlife tends to do. Early summer is the time to study the plant scene before the forest of hemlock and cow parsley takes over. Fortunately, the higher reaches of the Martin River, like my native Dallow and Allow, do not run through residential areas. Otherwise a variety of garden plants would have escaped to naturalise along the river banks. Some of these can be aggressively invasive.

Birds are by far the greatest of all seed propagators, particularly of any plant that produces fruits or berries. It is all part of nature's conspiracy to scatter the seeds by offering the berry as bait. As artificial vectors of seeds, both roads and railways also play a part. Unfortunately, on roads, with all that mud adhering to cars, it seems to be weeds that reap the benefit. The train seems to be more selective, particularly around Dublin where many gardens have bordered the line for generations. On every siding you will see the now naturalised monbretia (goldenrod), valerian (coax-the-ladies), buddleia (the butterfly tree) and other quite exotic blooms from faraway lands. These are welcome visitors.

The riverside has everything going for it – rich alluvial soil and natural irrigation. Whatever alien seed is deposited off the current has every chance of striking root. There is a downside to that. Really invasive weeds can readily establish themselves for miles along the flow of the water. We anglers know that all too well as we pass by once promising fishing stretches now choked and rendered useless. Balsam and pigweed, which spit their seeds quite a distance, are not at all welcome. Neither is the water buttercup and the pondweed, which choke rivers and lakes. The latter is now spreading rapidly in Killarney's lower lake and has choked great areas of Lough Corrib.

Worst of all the escapees is giant hogweed. It was introduced to gardens for its tall stature and beautifully sculptured acanthus leaves. What a plague it becomes once it gets near running water! It is highly toxic and once established is very difficult to control. The sap inflicts quite serious and chronic injury to tender skin and the use of the stem as a blowpipe is a fatal attraction for children. The plant has now infested the rivers around Nenagh and is working its way into the Shannon. Thank God it is not our problem down south as yet. Still, the very real threat is there.

One native plant, which is truly a noxious weed, is the bracken. Its fern fronds spread both by windblown spores and underground rhizomes. These thick, black feeding roots may spread at the astonishing rate of up to a metre per year. They have taken over not just rough terrain, but grazing land right through the country. In former times they were controlled both by frequent cutting when green in spring or by burning when dying in Autumn. This needed to be done on three consecutive years to achieve results, because the rhizomes store up energy to regenerate once left to themselves. Today we do not have that hands-on farm management of days past. The specific bracken herbicide called Asulam is costly and the application also needs to be repeated. Currently, experiments into discovering a biological control measure are underway. Meanwhile, it marches on inexorably. Its waist-height growth along riverbanks hampers the angler's cast. In recent years country dwellers have been made aware that the spores are carcinogenic.

I love the native flowers and the plants that still flourish around our streams. They seem to withstand a level of pollution that would wipe out fish life. One riverside plant which flourishes in April-May is the spurge, which we called *Bainne-na-nÉan* (the bird's milk). The light tender green of its first appearance is for me the colour of spring. The Irish name reflects the milky sap which pours out of the stems when crushed. It was a traditional treatment for warts. We knew that if you trampled a bundle at the head of a pool the fish came belly up – forgive us our trespasses. Later in the year we had the yellow flags or feilistrums. These served as casting spears when pitched battles took place around an Indian fort. 'Fond Mem'ry brings the light/Of other days around me'. When I now look at that yellow iris and the shy forget-me-not, which one commonly finds in quiet backwaters, the years fall away. There is a plant called bitter-sweet that well expresses those feelings of nostalgia. The name is a literal translation of the Greek *glukopikron*, which comes from its unusual flavour: sour when you first taste it and sweet when you chew it.

Laurens van der Post, in his magical book *The Heart of the Hunter*, describes with extraordinary insight the way of life of the aborigines in South Africa. The Bushmen have survived for millennia in the Kalahari Desert, totally dependent on the little that nature provides for basic sustenance. By our standard of living their world is primitive and harsh in the extreme. However, being in tune with the rhythms of Mother Nature, they enjoy a quality of life with which van der Post finds common ground. It is in total contrast with our consumerist culture, where fulfilment depends more and more on meeting the expectations of a technical man-made world. He sees us as restless, dissatisfied people in a culture where stress is endemic. One sentence of his sums it up: 'For the obsessed time stands still. They are cut off from the healing rhythm of the seasons'. Here the fishing rod should counteract that stress which is endemic in the modern way of life.

In all advanced countries there is an increasing response to the 'back to nature' call. Every Saturday, *The Irish Times* carries a column from Michael Viney, a respected journalist, who exchanged the pressure of Dublin life for the freedom of the Killary fjord and Mweelrea mountain in Mayo. Those from the cities who have taken up the option of family resettlement in Clare and other areas of the west have spoken of a similar sense of freedom in a culture that is relaxed and family friendly. They have traded a factor of standard of living for a major improvement in quality of life. They have realised that our society now marches to a drumbeat that is not in rhythm with human nature.

In the south-west counties there is an increasing number of business people in residence who work in Dublin,

London or wherever. Recently, walking my dogs in Schull, I stopped to admire the English setters of another walker. I presumed that he was on a late holiday because it was well outside the tourist season. He explained that he had his work done for the day. His office in London had downloaded yesterday's business overnight, which required his attention. He had dealt with it earlier and now the afternoon was his own. With a smile he said that the fibre optic cable and broadband would beat commuting through London traffic any day. I now know that many like him are enjoying the best of both worlds – earning a good living in the morning and breathing the sea air in the afternoon. They have found the elixir of life, that pearl of great price in the mind of the alchemists of olden times.

I once put it to an angling friend that we should advertise more widely the glories of the Irish countryside. Tongue-in-cheek he asked whether I had fallen out of my tree. If that kind of campaign succeeded the angling pattern on the riverbank would be 'standing room only'. We would need insurance against the risks of a false cast! I eased his fears by emphasising that the quotient of patience in our sport would rule it out for a new generation that demands quick results. Any thought of waiting around for action was not within their purview.

On a more serious vein, there is surely need to introduce young people to healthy physical exercise, as well as to appreciation and care for the environment. Former generations did not need to be concerned about the negative impacts of sedentary life. Obesity was not a problem when extra energy was burned off naturally. Addiction to PlayStations is toxic and the passivity induced by wall-to-wall televisions really does qualify it as chewing gum for the eyes. Is it any wonder that the main challenge for those who set out to train young people in competitive field sports today is to increase the level of basic fitness rather than perfect the standard of skill? We surely are sowing rouble for that new generation, which will bring a bitter harvest. Some years back a researcher did a comparative survey of a representative group of farmers in a region of Sliabh Lúacra, north Kerry, with their family members in Boston. The solid meals of bacon and cabbage along with the absence of stress and plenty of physical exercise saw the men of Sliabh Lúacra into their nineties, long after their Boston relatives were in their graves.

I believe that some modern-style houses inserted into rural settings are quite out of place. As time goes on nature will soften their contours, provided native trees shade them from view. Modern technology in any form does not marry with the rural environment. This came to mind recently when I asked an elderly neighbour how iron bars used in fencing had been welded into the rocks. It emerged that a one-inch hole had been drilled into the stone and a mixture of molten sulphur and coarse sand would then lock the bar into position. The weld held firm far more effectively than the leaden fixing more frequently employed. What ingenuity! How was it discovered? Another mystery of the countryside.

When one compares in human terms the modern world of technology with the original world of nature, the former comes across as sterile and restricting. Its focus is to hone the intellect and transmit technical know-how. The world of nature is where the complete human person is schooled. It provides an outreach towards a healthy emotional balance. Its easy rhythm is a balm, an antidote to depression that is downwind of stress. Furthermore, it situates the spiritual at the heart of a positive philosophy of life. When I visited an old friend, who had been sixty years in religion, I would invariably find him of a fine evening beside a water feature in the monastery garden. In response to my observation, he recalled that in the Adam and Eve creation story it is said that God would walk in the Garden of Eden in the cool of the day. What better place then to find Him than in a garden? That old friend had been a keen angler. He also knew a great deal about the curative powers of plants, pointing out that caring for the monastery garden as well as serving the fish weir would once have been key duties of the monks.

The monastery garden has a long tradition. A major section of that garden would have been the herbarium with an extensive selection of medicinal and culinary herbs. On the healing qualities of those herbs, some monks would be expert in identifying the indications for their use and the proper method of prescribing. At a time when hospitals as we now know them were not in existence, the monasteries and abbeys provided a very important service to patients. There was no shortage of medicinal herbs in the countryside. That is clear from Niall Mac Coitir's most informative book, *Irish Wild Plants: Myths, Legends and Folklore.* The use of curative herbs as alternative medicine not alone still continues, but is coming more into vogue. Seán Boylan, trainer of the Meath football team, as a herbalist is famed for his skill in this field. Perhaps the fitness of those famed footballers owes something to this hidden knowledge.

Hospitals are now introducing gardens as part of the holistic healing process. The environment of a garden and running water is therapeutic, as opposed to the confinement of a hospital ward and the clinical atmosphere in the institution generally. Again it endorses the reality of a psychosomatic factor in the process of healing and recovery after a traumatic experience. This positive influence on emotions and through the emotions on the whole person is particularly important in psychiatric units, something which surely stands to reason on its own, without the need for further proof from the modern science of holistic medicine.

When it comes to angling, I know that for some colleagues the verdict on the success of the day is to be read in the size of the bag. For true anglers, there is far more to it than that. They will read the Book of Nature and make common cause with the range of interest which it provides. I accept that the Rural Environmental Protection Scheme (REPS), through the financial incentive in its grant aid, is a welcome help towards sustaining the farming community in rural Ireland. For farmers who love their land there is far more to caring for it than the grant incentive requires. They will take pride in managing that land to achieve its potential as a form of nature reserve. This is what I admire in the recent initiative by the local community of Rathcormac in East Cork – a positive policy to preserve the natural environment and establish wild flower meadows. It is of interest to know that many of the most active members of the group are anglers. That is no surprise to me.

~ 3. From Worm to Fly

Every young angler makes his or her debut trotting a worm along the current into a likely pool in the hope that a fish is waiting. The inclusive 'his' or 'her' may seem redundant, but angling is no respecter of gender. The earliest book in English on fishing as a sport was written by a Dame Juliana Berners in 1496. To my chagrin, on one of our early outings to the Dallow a young sister of mine took up my rod, cast the worm bait at random into the pool beside the Black Bridge and hooked a trout over a pound in weight. Beginner's luck, you may well say, but I was not allowed to forget it. I have known a few women who became lifelong sisters of the angle. I lavished fulsome praise on one of them for her nimble fingers in tying the neatest trout flies imaginable. Praise got the results. Some prototypes of her lures I still treasure. Of course, the exception proves the rule. Most anglers are men because in them the hunter instinct is stronger.

Let us stay with the worm for a while even though purists dismiss it as beneath contempt. Worms vary in the angler's book. The bluehead holds pride of place when the river is murky with flood water. The best blueheads in my memory were to be found in the ground behind a haybarn where ashes and cinders had blended with the debris of the haggard. These were tough and lively to the extent of being almost fit to catch fish on their own, as one confident angler said. The next choice was the smaller red bramblings that were to be found in sandy loam on the riverbank. These worked well in clear water.

Amateurs might judge that the common or garden earthworm would provide a good-sized bite for a fish. We called them 'hags'. To avoid labour with the spade an angler would steal upon them with a flashlamp at night, particularly on a damp lawn. They might be blind but they kept their ends securely anchored in their tunnels, ready for lightning withdrawal at the slightest vibration on the ground. Another trick was to spray the ground with detergent so as to drive them to the surface. For the genuine angler it was hardly worth the bother. At best the hags would bulk up the bait when one fished for salmon with a ball of worms, but they would quickly disintegrate off the hook.

There is an ancient Irish proverb which cautions one to be always ready in good time for any emergency: *Ní hé lá na gaoithe lá na scolb*. With the storm already blowing is no time to be cutting the scollops for thatching. The same applies about going to gather worms with the river in flood. The keen angler will have the worms ready in stock so as to be all set when the call comes. The traditional way of holding them in readiness for that call was the largest earthenware flower pot available filled with damp, sandy loam and buried in the shade away from the sun. The drainage hole in the base would be blocked with a cork and a piece of sacking stretched firmly as a cover. One would dampen the sacking and add some lawn cuttings on top of the contents underneath.

From this cache of hardy worms, the angler on the way to the river would choose some to be placed in damp moss in something like a cocoa tin with a perforated lid. The half-pound jam jar might seem equally serviceable, but glass has

risks. A Blackwater angler met his tragic death after a fall
on the riverbank when such a jam jar splintered and severed
a main leg artery. It was a singular accident in anyone's
book but it lived on in the memory of the local anglers.

To an outsider, sliding a worm over a hook and dropping
it into a pool of water may seem simplicity itself. To catch
fish demands a lot more skill in the use of the right tactics.
One must judge a promising lie for a feeding trout and then
'trot' the bait naturally down the current. Presentation is
everything at this final stage. In moving up to the ambush,
from behind the fish if possible, one keeps a low profile, taking advantage of every bit of cover. This will not be necessary in murky flood water, but as the colour clears it
becomes a necessity. For this kind of worm fishing the
tackle may be rough and ready with the river in full flood. I
well recall a neighbour who would slip away from work in
the meadow, tie a length of fishing line to the handle of the
hay rake, bait a hook with a worm and take up station at his
favourite whirlpool where he knew that trout would congregate. In that company I felt quite comfortable with my
hazel rod.

Clear water worm fishing is not as common a practice in
Ireland as in Britain. It would require a proper fishing rod to
land a worm precisely ahead of where fish might lie. Those
little red worms, which are called bramblings, were then the
bait of choice. Presenting that bait without disturbing the
water in front was a refined skill. It certainly rated higher in
terms of game fishing than our cruder practice.

Closest to the clear water worm was our system of minnow fishing. Minnows or collies were plentiful at the time.
What suited the minnow was our good fortune that the
Dallow quite surprisingly was a limestone river. Quite surprisingly at that, because its many minor feeder rivulets

were acid bog streams. What made the difference was the fine deepwater spring that erupted from the bed of limestone, which ran under Meelin village. This now supplies water over a large area of north-west Cork's towns and villages so that the overflow into the river is sadly depleted. That generous limestone spring of days past was known as the Blessed Well. Why so called no one seemed to know, beyond the tinge of red on its pebbles. It certainly was a blessing for us anglers as limestone water is ideal for healthy fish growth. In the deep pool a few hundred yards below the Black Bridge we would watch those long-lived trout, relative monsters in our eyes, lazily circling around. We tried everything in the book to strokehaul and snare them with a horsehair loop when all conventional methods had failed. We then came to appreciate why they were long- lived.

The minnows, which require clear limestone water in which to thrive, would have been shoaling in every quiet backwater. Curiosity was their downfall. Coaxing them into a jam jar was as simple a matter as taking a worm from a blind hen, to quote one man's colourful language. When fitted with very fine tackle they served as live bait and grassed many a fine trout blessed with that good taste, which would have scorned a common or garden worm. The minnows in the Dallow are no more. The limestone supply from the Blessed Well has been siphoned off to such an extent that the flow under the Black Bridge, apart from a spate in flood, is now just a trickle of the ordinary surface water of the locality. That stream drains a catchment area which leaves it exposed to farm and domestic waste. When I last inspected it, the floating suds and smears of tell-tale froth told their own story, a story far too common in Ireland today. I assume that the source of the Blessed Well itself is no longer pristine clean. Unlike the percolation factor in shale and sandstone, of which there is plenty in the wider Meelin area, limestone does not filter the underground water which sluices straight through the divisions and fissures into the surface springs.

Thank God for the memories that are still clear. One of my happiest reminiscences is attached to fishing with the woodbee, more commonly known in angling literature as the woodfly. This blue-bottle sized fly was then plentiful. It was attracted to fresh horse dung. A box would be triggered to drop over the flies *in situ* and then through a small hole on top of the box they would exit single file into a bottle. When threaded on a tiny hook with a fine gut one was ready to attract the biggest fish in the eye of a whirlpool. Keeping back out of sight was essential. The cautious approach would usually find its reward in a swirl as the fish rose to take the fly. The secret was to allow a few seconds for the trout to turn down before one tightened up on the strike. A rushed spontaneous reaction left you with a bare hook and a scared fish. It was agreed that no other bait could beat the woodbee when it came to catching those big trout on the right day.

That was the final step for us in live bait angling. To advance further, you hoisted the hazel rod to the rafters in memory of old times. You had hoped that a generous parent would read the signs and buy you a proper split cane rod. This surely did the business on graduating to casting the artificial fly. Of course nowadays a young angler would not be seen dead on the river with a hazel rod. All the tackle must be top-of-the-range and state-of-the-art. Parents are indulgent with the cost in the hope that a son will take up a healthy outdoor sport rather than become a layabout prone to fall in with the wrong sort. I think that the hazel rod played an important role in building up angling skills for the beginner. If you learn to cast bait neatly with the hazel you will be master of the art with the split cane. An added bonus for the beginner is that the hazel will survive a bout of rough handling which would shatter a more fragile rod.

The dry fly fishing with the oiled floating fly is celebrated in the great chalk streams of Britain. For British anglers, on those special waters anything else would be judged obscene and a sacrilege. There, all the art is in stalking your fish and casting your fly, ending with a neat flick to float it gently into the taking ground. For that the artificial fly in size and colour must be well nigh identical with the natural ones which are on the water at the time. Even with the same fly species one must distinguish between the newly hatched 'dun' and the egg-laying 'spent'. Those chalk stream trout are most choosy and discriminating. They merit the most exquisite skills of master anglers. I watched one expert fishing the Wye near Tintern Abbey on an evening made for the dry fly. What an art! I concluded that any similarity between his efforts and mine were purely coincidental.

In Ireland we generally favour on our rivers the wet or sunken fly. This imitates the underwater hatching nymph or the drowned mature fly in its many stages. Even though the size, shape and colour of fly is still important, those factors are not as critical as they are for the dry fly. In the Dallow and Allow, our staple flies through most of the year, when the river olives were on the wing, would have been the Greenwell's Glory, the Red Spinner and the Wickham's Fancy. In the autumn, with the sedges on the water, we would favour the Alder above all others. This was known popularly as the Rail, tied traditionally with the feathers from the corncrake, in angling literature commonly called the land rail in contrast to the water rail, which is more generally known as the water hen.

We might have a fly box filled with a selection of other specimens with names to conjure with, but we would generally stay with the old tried and tested reliables. Anglers act in character here. Let them browse in a fish tackle shop and they will come out with far more flies than will ever see the water. Looking at them and turning them over in the fly box gives vicarious satisfaction and in terms of therapy is the very stuff of dreams as the season is about to roll.

There is no greater satisfaction than tying one's own flies and enjoying the thrill of catching fish with them. Here again one could have to hand a stock of more raw materials than would decorate a tackle shop. Cape of bronze bantam cock, wing of teal and blue jay, peacock herl, golden pheasant tippet, hare's ear, badger hackle, stoat's tail etc. – that is just a few of the traditional natural materials. It sounds like the recipe for the witches' brew in Shakespeare's *Macbeth*. I spent many a happy evening in the home of my dear friends Jim and Rosalie O'Callaghan at Bárr-na-Féile in Duagh on the Feale as we tied salmon and sea trout flies. They were carefree days and have left good memories. Those memories come back when I visit a group of keen youngsters in Mallow under the guidance of local anglers, honing their skills in tying flies and lures for the Blackwater. It reminded me of young days when we used every chance to provide materials for fly tying. The bronze feathers on the cape of a neighbour's bantam cock attracted our interest. We grabbed the opportunity when the neighbour had gone for his usual few pints to the local pub. When he noticed the plucked neck of his prize bird the following morning he concluded that the cock had a close encounter with some predator.

Once you get into experimenting with artificial fibres there is no end in sight. The best nymph lure I created for

evening buzzer fishing on the great midland lakes was a
hook simply fitted with a black silk thread body, headed
with a few twists of orange fibre from the plastic ribbon
that then bound packets of peat briquettes. Inevitably the
result was christened the Lullymore. It brought in the
biggest fish as a matter of course when they were on the
move late of a calm evening.

A dedicated fly tier will go to any lengths to secure the
wherewithal for his craft. Beg, borrow or steal. It is
reported that as a parish priest of Duagh on the river Feale
surveyed the congregation at a Sunday Mass, he stopped
dead in mid-sentence during the sermon. He had observed a
visitor home from the States with a hat festooned with
exotic feathers. As Mass ended he asked that she come
around to the sacristy, declaring an interest in the hat. The
locals rightly surmised his intent and put the embarrassed
woman at her ease. His sharp eye had identified the scarlet
feathers of the Indian Crow holding pride of place on that
hat. As a dedicated salmon angler he surmised that this
addition to the Bloody Butcher might make it just the lure
for fresh run grilse on the Feale. I have been told that on
St Patrick's Day, on the opening of the salmon season on
the Feale, the parish priest had the privilege of being first on
the river. One informant told me that the sacristan would be
commissioned to police the church door to secure that no
angler in the congregation broke ranks until the priest had
donned his fishing gear in the sacristy after Mass.

I cannot recall that any angler on the Dallow was seriously into the fly tying business. The tried and tested shop
patterns from Day's in Cork worked well enough and there
was no call for novelties. Perhaps Rory Sheehan, a retired
bank clerk and a keen angler, might well have been into
experimentation. He was not the kind of character to

divulge any of his secrets. In any case, we youngsters avoided him because he treated the Dallow as his particular fiefdom. Perhaps he suspected that our methods of capturing fish were not always above board. In that suspicion he might well be right.

Lateral thinking was second nature to us. If there are fish in a pool there must be some way of extracting them. The challenge must be met or else we lose self-respect. A night line was often effective. All it needed was a hook baited with a worm and the line left in the pool overnight in the hope that, come morning, a big trout would have obliged. More often than not an eel would have beaten him to it. We had no time for eels. We saw them as pests, messy pests at that when it came to retrieving a buried hook. For us they had nothing to offer to life in the stream. Later I gained more respect for them when I learned about their extraordinary emigration pattern. It required a long ocean voyage to the Saragossa Sea to lay their eggs among the mat of seaweed that spreads on the surface. From there the elvers returned to our rivers. We had indeed observed these elvers, little thicker than a horse-hair, but we had not then realised that these were the young eels.

The full-grown eels we met in the Dallow would have been at best around eighteen inches in length. Those in the Feale were larger. It was only when I came to fish the midland lakes of Sheelin, Ennell and Derravaragh that I saw monsters as long as an oar and over four inches in diameter. No wonder there are Gaelic stories about the *ollpéist* to rival the accounts of Scotland's Loch Ness Monster. Years ago there used to be a thriving eel export business in Ireland based on the great migration of the fully mature silver eels on their way to spawn. The Lough Neagh fishery was a very valuable industry in harvesting these eels. Jellied eel was a delicacy, particularly in France and Germany. I never had the wish to try it. My memory of those messy creatures in the Dallow had spoiled my taste.

Anyway, back to trout and lateral thinking on ways to trap them. We had come to know of the practice of 'tickling' trout in smaller streams where fish would take shelter under the bank for security and shelter. They would lay there, semi-dormant, head forward, tail back. A quiet soundless approach was essential because any vibration on the ground carries through the water. Then one would lie down, slip a hand out into the pool and feel along under the bank. The slow beat of a fish tail might then be sensed. Now a gentle tickle underneath would act like a welcome massage to the semi-dormant trout as it backs gradually out of its holt. A quick tighten between thumb and forefinger will do the rest.

Personally, I was not very keen on the practice. It may be a myth but one that certainly widely circulated to the effect that some unfortunate had grabbed a rat in the process. I put all my reservations to the side on one occasion when I saw a fine trout feeding greedily on flies in a tiny pool under a road culvert at Poul-a-Dash below Meelin village. It would not qualify as a real pool but that trout had made it his station. Off with shoes and stockings and into the water to feel through the divisions among the masonry for any tell-tale flick of a fish tail. There it was, barely perceptible. The trout responded in the standard fashion and I landed a well-nourished fish just over a pound in weight.

That set us thinking. Suppose we actually made an attractive shelter for the trout in a large well-stocked pool? We then excavated an underwater tunnel on a loop with two entrances into the pool about three yards apart. Now we were in business. With a homemade net over the exit point we disturbed the water at the other end to flush the fish through. To preserve the stock we might take just the few bigger ones. Anyway, it is a proven fact that if a larger fish vacates his station in the river, another moves in to take its place. Our scheme was not unlike the custom canals that wildfowl hunters used a century ago to drive ducks into the narrowing end covered with a net. There they were trapped.

We tried every trick that took our fancy. The riverside spurge has a white juice which was known to be toxic to fish. I have already spoken of how we would gather bundles of them and tread them on the current into a pool. It didn't work well, presumably because the volume of water had diluted the white extract. Having experimented with every strategy that we had learned from others or could invent for ourselves we were back to the rod and line. This was true sport and set the seed for a lifetime of enjoyment.

4. The Great Midland Lakes ⌒

In the 1960s, shortly after my appointment to the post in the Faculty of Theology in Maynooth, I made the acquaintance of Loughs Ennell, Sheelin, Owel and Arrow. Here was the quality of fishing that one had read about in anglers' diaries of days past. The chain of lakes in the Mullingar region are limestone based and rich in the staple food for big trout. This was evident as clouds of flies in the mating dance rose like chimneys over the alders that ringed the lakes. The trout averaged two pounds or so with a fair scatter of monsters over double that weight. An hour in the car from Maynooth to Butler's Bridge, just beyond Mullingar, saw one ready for action in the boat on Lough Ennell. Fr Brendan Devlin, Professor of Modern Languages in Maynooth, was my partner on many a happy outing. Lough Ennell is quite a shallow lake all over and you need little guidance on where to fish. Some places still stand out in memory. Belvedere, the Burrow Hill, the Keoltown Reeds, Goose Island – all names to conjure with. In Herbert Maxwell's *Angling Theories and Methods,* I had read of the splendid trout of Loch Leven, close to Dundee in Scotland. That book was written eighty years ago. Those silvery native lake trout were celebrated as the finest in Britain in game fishing and had often been used to stock other waters. When I visited that loch some years ago it was a poor shadow of what it must have been. The boats moored at Kinross seemed neglected. I think that even at its best it would not have competed with the sport on our midland lakes. On going to fish the loch with a local angler, he sadly explained that Leven had now been stocked from a commercial rainbow trout hatchery. The silvery wild trout of legend were a memory.

Later on I will deal expressly with the highlights of the mayfly fishing in the Irish midland lakes, but there was so much else in which to glory. The only flat time was in July when the perch fry were everywhere in huge shoals. The trout would gorge on these. A shoal of trout would dash through the reed beds to drive out the fry and then feed on them voraciously like mackerel after sprat on the seashore. The odds were stacked against any chance of an angler's lure having success among those myriads of perch fry. Apart from that flat period for fly fishing, one could always be quite sure that one would not have a blank day. Lake olives and buzzers were always in good supply through the summer months and there were many artificial imitations tied on standard size ten hooks. The Connemara Black, the Black Pennell, Watson's Fancy, the Fiery Brown and what-ever else your option was on the day might also do the busi-ness. Everyone had their favourites and confidence in one's cast of flies was everything. That confidence made for more serious fishing.

We must not forget the Duck Fly, which was first to appear in vast numbers in the spring. You would see reefs of them washed up on the shore after a good hatch out in the lake. Again the great numbers that were available on the water constituted a problem for the hopeful angler. Later on a larger cousin of the Duck Fly, known properly as the St Mark's Fly, would blow out off the shore. This was a sub-stantial black fly with long hanging legs. I had come to know it in the Killarney lakes as well. It was a glorious sight to see fish coming head-and-tail for it as it plumped on the water. The Black Pennell was the favourite lure.

After the mayfly season had ended, the buzzer appeared. This looks like a large gnat and its name describes its action on the water. In the calm of the evening, one would have fished with a floating line and furry imitation of the natural type. With that dry fly we would catch a trout or two. An angler from the Corrib dismissed us with our dry flies and on a lake surface of mirror calm would catch fish on the ordinary wet flies, to which he was accustomed at home. The patterns he used were the Sooty Olive and the Claret and Mallard. Evidently the fish saw these under the water as buzzer nymphs. Dan Goldrick, Area Superintendent of the Inland Fisheries Trust, who was on the way out to fish Lough Ennell on the evening rise, let me in on the secret. I decided to experiment with buzzer nymphs and produced the above mentioned Lullymore. The fishing method on calm water was a matter of easing the boat along until you observed a fish feeding solidly, head-and-tail in shallow water. Then you cast ahead of him and moved the nymph very gently under the surface. The take would be literally ferocious. In that shallow water the fish would run for the deep and set the reel smoking. That was fishing indeed.

On an occasion, when our boat had been set adrift by some young fellow fishing for perch, I borrowed the next boat in line to go out to retrieve it. I had the rod already set up, pulled on the Wellingtons and did not bother to bail the boat, which was half full of water. As I pulled out slowly on the calm lake, I observed a large trout feeding solidly just ahead. The water-logged boat moved sluggishly but just quickly enough to get into position for a lucky cast. This was as fine a trout as ever I hooked. But no landing net on board! Another boat came across and handed me a net for the final act of the drama, or so I thought. In that concept of final act I was mistaken. The character in the boat, having photographed the action, saw an opportunity to put a spin on the story. I featured in the next edition of the local paper almost up to my knees in water with the rod bent in the fish. The storyline ran: 'Angler proves that the best way to keep a low profile in approaching a feeding fish on a calm lake is to fill the boat half full of water'. That is how fisherman's tales are inflated after the event.

When Brendan Devlin and I made the acquaintance of Fr Mattie Coleman and Oliver Buckley of Mullingar, we had ready access to Lough Sheelin. They had a well-appointed army surplus Nissan hut right on the shore with a slipway for their boats. Lough Sheelin was of the same quality as Ennell but far greater in extent. When it came to the mayfly season this was the choice of anglers after Ennell. With drainage work on the Brosna river the water level in Ennell had dropped considerably. This had severely affected the mayfly hatch there, even though the Ennell Preservation Association along with the Inland Fisheries Trust had done Trojan work in re-establishing it. In our time, anglers still recalled securing mature mayfly from Lough Derravaragh and transporting them to Ennell in muslin-lined tea chests.

The technical name for the mayfly is *Ephemera danica*. Ephemeral it certainly is with its short existence after emergence from the water to mate and lay its eggs. It is the very breath of summer, rising from the murky depths to become a water sprite. It is just so beautiful as it flutters ashore on gossamer wings to lodge on the lakeside bushes. The anglers know it at this stage as the Green Drake and collect it as bait for dapping. When it comes to lay its eggs on warm evenings and falls to die on the surface of the water it is called the Spent Gnat. This makes for superb dry fly fishing with the artificial fly. Some purists consider this true mayfly angling and scorn the dapping duffers with their long bamboo poles. Those purists of the Spent might deign to fish the mayfly nymph or even the artificial dry mayfly, but dapping the natural would be quite beneath them – the equivalent of worm fishing on a chalk stream.

Still it is the dapping fraternity who go into a frenzy of summer madness when news comes down the line, 'Fly is up!' For weeks the anticipation will have ratcheted up the excitement to the level of what nuclear scientists would call 'critical mass'. Outboard motors will have been serviced and diaries cleared. Nothing would be allowed to stand in the way of the countdown to ground zero. They will have the tackle all set and ready for the off. The long bamboo dapping pole, or the fibreglass telescopic rod, the silk floss blow-line to carry the dapped fly out in the breeze ahead of the boat, the ventilated wooden box for holding the live mayflies – readying all this is what dreams are made of. In the mind's eye they can see the Green Drake on its diaphanous lace wings rising off the water light as a feather while the breeze wafts it ashore. They will sense the soft west wind setting up a rolling wave against a background of mixed sun and cloud.

In the dream they will picture rising fish throwing up plumes of spray as they scoop up the flies hatching ahead of the drifting boat. Then the tension as one waits in hope for the explosion when a large fish may select one's bait in pref-erence to the others afloat on the wave. In this event, the shock to the system will be severe. It may even prove fatal, as on one occasion an ancient angler keeled over with the shock. However, first things first! The story goes that his companion took up the rod and played the fish to the net before attending to the casualty! His comment afterwards was, 'Well, didn't he die happy!'

Even in a less eventful situation, prayer has a part to play in the strike action. Every dapper is warned to wait for some time after the fish has taken the fly before one strikes the hook home. It is a matter of precise timing of the strike until the fish has turned down after the take. Some old hands recommended delaying the strike through the first verse of the Hail Mary – or at the very least through the first phrase of the Glory be to the Father. It is reported that an Englishman out with an Irish boatman would delay the strike while he slowly chanted, 'God save the Queen'. The boatman would solemnly pronounce, '*Go méadaigh Dia ár stór*'. Disloyal as he felt, the Englishman admitted that the Irish mantra worked the better. You may still miss the strike whichever mantra you put your trust in. In that case, the appropriate response depends on the black depths of your mood at the time. One should never forget that sound carries verbal irritation far over water!

'Oft in the stilly night,/Ere slumber's chain has bound me,/Fond Mem'ry brings the light/Of other days around me' (Thomas Moore). In days past, when mayfly mania was at its height, God forbid that anything or anyone should stand in the way of having those dreams realised. To most people, May suggests a quiet, restful month when nature decks herself out in her summer leisure wear and relaxes as swallows circle and the cuckoo calls. Not so for those anglers to whom the great midland and western lakes drum an insistent message. Loughs Corrib, Mask and Carra, Sheelin, Ennell and Owel may conjure up gentle, happy memories during the long, depressing winter months. Come May, that generalised nostalgia gives way to straightforward mania. These same men are now champing at the bit, waiting for the magic words, 'Fly is up!' The reaction is near relative to that rutting season which brute creatures experience. During this period of waiting, anglers are a particularly dangerous lot. Tempers are on a very short fuse. The male of the species starts throwing up grass on slight provocation. Family members are well advised to discover pressing business elsewhere when father starts to get his tackle together. They sensibly leave the disease to run its two-week course. Perhaps someone has stretched up the precious three-piece dapping rod to poke down the cobwebs from the corners of the landing in preparation for the Station Mass. It has been known to happen! The non-angler does not always realise how fragile rod tips and top rings are. When the sad results of that sacrilegious use are discovered, the victim is best left to vent his frenzy in private.

At least in that situation one can focus blame on a third party, some family miscreant as yet unknown. Imagine the horror when one discovers that a predatory moth has fostered a progeny of voracious larvae in one's box of special mayfly tyings. Mosley Green Drakes, Goslings, Blue Devils, Spent Gnats, Grey Dusters – all chomped to dust and ashes before one's unbelieving eyes. I have seen it happen. I have known a strong man on the brink of tears in face of such ruin – with no one but himself to blame. The problem is that here you have a free-floating, all-consuming rage which comes home to roost solidly on one's own carelessness. Never did the words of Jesus ring so true: 'Lay not up your treasure where rust and moth destroy'. One then knows all about that remorse which the Monaghan poet Patrick Kavanagh called the Devil's contrition – 'What an idiot I was not to have fastened that fly box tightly!' One looks for a potentially liable third party, someone maybe who should have placed camphor moth balls in the wardrobe when those fly boxes were stored.

You can imagine how nerves are frayed to breaking point by the time a trusted lakeside contact phones to say, 'Fly is up!' Depending on the prevailing warmth of the weather, the call can come anytime between mid-May and early June. Once it comes, the Gadarene gallop is on. Wife and children are summarily abandoned. Work schedules are scrubbed or re-arranged. The professional classes are particularly prone to the contagion. When hospital theatre staff note that wild glint in a surgeon's eye, they know that his urgent operation list will be covered in record time, with everything except emergency cases put back for later attention. In the law courts, counsel are quick to spot the growing impatience of judges. Any false move or delaying tactic could qualify as contempt of court. The learned legal friends in attendance would take the point well because they too might be planning to join him in the lemming-like exodus to the west.

The mayfly season coincides with the bloom of the mayflower, as the midlanders called the hawthorn. Along the lush fields around Mullingar, every fence is lined with flowering hawthorn. Not that the speeding anglers from Dublin have much time to admire the scenery. They are hell bent on getting to the lakes. On one occasion, as I was on the road to Mullingar with boat in tow, an impatient angler passed me out with a saluting flourish on the horn. Speed with anything in tow can occasion a wobble. With a boat you are in double jeopardy because the air lift under the bow can float the boat off the trailer. In the passing-out manouevre, this is exactly what occurred. In the collision with the roadside wall the rib cage of the boat opened out like an umbrella. I had the role of Good Samaritan as I lodged his paraphernalia into my boat and took good care to make everything ship shape.

Of course, the early birds would be the envy of all others as they had been able to take off on the spur of the word. For them, Lough Derg on the Shannon was destination of first choice. There the mayfly came earliest. It ideally suited me and some Maynooth colleagues because the revision period for the students was scheduled for mid-May. That left us the best part of a fortnight before we were back on duty for the examinations. I never did find out whether this timely break had been inspired by more than academic considerations. I have happy memories of Lough Derg with the Minogue Hotel in Scariff and the McMahon family in Woodford. May the Lord grant them all the light of heaven.

When one makes it to the lake shore, it is every man for himself. People who are generally the very soul of concern and generosity now become tight-lipped and stony hearted. Requests for a spare rowlock or landing net may simply not register. Such requests cannot penetrate the compulsive, obsessive mentality that has now overcome the ordinarily rational psyche. And as for sharing local knowledge of where the best hatch of mayfly is expected, or where the rise of trout was encountered yesterday, forget it. Take it as a useful rule of thumb to do the opposite of what you are told. No one really tells lies because no one expects to be believed anyway. Indeed, the Roman collar may help to get the truth because one's destiny may suffer a setback if one crosses a priest at the start of the day.

With today's ease of travel, the mayfly exodus does not have the same expeditionary quality of days past. It has become a more haphazard affair where anglers almost commute to and from the lakes, depending on the quality of fishing. In days past, one settled in for the duration, dapping the natural fly by day and casting the artificial at dusk. Anglers left home loaded with gear as for a campaign to Everest. Everything was carried in case something was needed. The consequence was that teeth would be grinding with impatience as a colleague took time to sort through all that tackle as the boat was set to launch.

I well recall during the 1960s the diverse team of characters that gathered year-in, year-out on the Shannon at the homely Minogue Hotel at Scariff in Clare. Legal and medical men mostly – not a woman in sight nor in mind. Professional prestige or technical expertise counted for nothing. Angling skill was the great leveller and the amateur competitors would have traded a full week's income for a good day's catch. Stories were swapped at late-night meals of great fish risen but not hooked, hooked and played to the net but not landed. The two Minogue sisters did not stand on ceremony. At whatever time you made it home you raided the kitchen and took potluck, and here no one was ever known to draw a blank. After a day on the lake, it was a case of skipping the trimmings of *haute cuisine* and getting to solid fare.

Year after year the usual suspects would be in residence, with 'outliers' bedded around the village. The term 'outliers' originally referred to stags adrift off the deer park. It was applied to these outside guests by a Highland laird who seemed to spend all his days salmon fishing, grouse shooting or deer stalking. He had a big booming voice which signified someone to the manor born. However, everyone was kept in place by a figure of quiet authority with few words, a judge of the High Court. Even the Highlander answered Amen to his pronouncements. Whatever one's walk of life – be it judge, surgeon, banker or cleric – the craze of the mayfly was still the great leveller that welded them into a single species. What counted was prowess in the boat, not authority on the bench. In the group there had been some characters before my time and their fame long outlived them. The exploits of a pair of brothers remained in the annals. Their love-hate relationship in the boat was proverbial. It was said that in the excitement of playing a fish one lost his dentures overboard. The other planned a stratagem. While he was landing a trout he dropped his own dentures into the net and then announced to the incredulity of the other that he had rescued the lost dentures! One wag added a codicil to the story that, having tried the allegedly lost dentures in his mouth, the other threw them overboard in disgust!

When the day was over on the lake the banter around the dinner table was an experience. As a young man I was happy to listen and indulge my seniors. I do not remember too many of the stories because I would have been too drowsy after the day on the lake. I do recall a story about a bishop and judge as power brokers. It was told by the Highlander as having happened centuries back on the border circuit. The bishop, who was host as usual, put it to the judge that he was the more powerful because he could proclaim 'be damned' while all the judge could pronounce was 'be hanged'. 'Aye,' said the judge, 'but when I pronounce it the man ends up hanged – whereas you don't know'.

A priest was always welcome in that company because it was an unwritten rule that an early Mass would be provided for the angling fraternity, whatever their individual affiliation. During the ceremony one might observe weather eyes focusing on the sky to see how cloud was building up and whether the wind rate was increasing to provide the right conditions. A calm sunny day was bad news. Quite often the May weather would be harsh and stormy. This was *scairbhín na gcuac*, the rough weather at the time of the cuckoo's arrival, but that wind and rain would not deter the mayfly angler. One member of the group in the Scariff hotel recalled how a legendary dapper recalled that the best day he ever had was out with two gillies, one on the oars and the other bailing the boat!

Bliss it was in those days to be alive; to be young was very heaven! While the hawthorn draped the Tipperary shore of Lough Derg, the Clare shore blazed with furze. What a paradise for anyone with a sense of wonder! The clouds of mayfly rising off the lake and floating ashore to festoon any available tree for a few short days before laying their eggs and dying in the effort. I share with Brendan Devlin the memory of our hospitable accommodation in the Burke farmhouse at Scarriff. What I recall is that spreading hawthorn tree in full bloom filling the yard with its scent. It was a totem presiding over the mayfly season.

Once the mayfly got really underway we were spoiled for choice on the midland lakes. It was a matter of tossing a coin. In the west, Corrrib, Mask, Carra and Conn beckoned. Nearer home were Sheelin, Ennell, Derravaragh, Owel and Arrow. '*Ni féider leis an gobadán and dá tráth a fhreastail*' - no sand piper can feed on two strands. Naturally we were reluctant to pass the midland lakes. We were familiar with them and we had boats to hand. Furthermore, on Sheelin our angling friends had that Nissan hut all geared out on the very shores of the lake. There one could fish the evening, rise late as one wished and cook a meal without being time-bound.

Reliving those happy days is it any wonder that nostalgia tracks down memory lane! Talking of the mayfly, one evening stands out for me as exceptional. A local general practitioner, Dr Tom McMahon, and I were returning in the calm of the evening into Mountshannon on Lough Derg when we noted a large trout feeding on spent mayfly now expiring on the water. Cutting the engine, I rowed him within range. In less than a minute the water exploded as he struck. It was dark before we landed ten pounds of a mighty trout. All around, homing anglers rested on their oars as they watched the battle. That night the competition in Minogue's hotel in Scarriff were dumbstruck. Even the Highlander stroked his beard in silence as he weighed up the result of a lucky strike.

On the mayfly front, things ain't what they used to be. Glorious Lough Derg on the Shannon lost its red letter status in the fishing calendar. The drift of peat debris from the Bord na Móna workings had choked the gravel spawning grounds and had laid down a layer of bog stuff over the limestone bed of the lake. As if that were not enough, an unwelcome arrival is the zebra mussel, which may have imported itself via Limerick. That simply sheets the floor of the lake and radically alters the sensitive balance of the ecosystem. One result is the thorough filtration of the water as the mussels feed on algae. The good news is that 2007 has shown an improvement.

Then the midland lakes have been hit by pollution on a large scale. The term eutrophication, overnourishment, masks the nature of the damaging agent. It was chiefly due to domestic effluent from Mullingar into Lough Ennell and pig slurry from Cavan into Lough Sheelin. Over and above, there is the nitrate/phosphate run-off from farmland. Unfortunately, the geography of Ireland's saucer shape means that our draining rivers run slow and allow algae to build up in inland waters. The fertilizer drives a vast bloom of algae in hot weather. Water is starved of oxygen. It means that angling is seriously compromised. This is particularly true in regard to the mayfly. It is the largest of the olive family of flies which flourish in limestone rivers and lakes. This family is highly vulnerable to deterioration in water quality. So its demise sends a signal which we ignore at serious cost to the environment.

Currently a good deal of work is being done to improve the quality of water in the midland lakes. The mayfly summer madness should again mark time in red lettering in the angler's diary. Of course, mayfly or no, we should not forget the superb autumn fishing with the Green Peter and the Murrough. These great sedges were the speciality on Lough Owel. Anglers would sit quietly in their boats awaiting the rise of the Peters on a warm August evening along the Portloman shore. The sight of herring gulls dipping and feeding off the water was the sign. The large artificial sedge dry fly would have been oiled and ready on the rod. Another would be clipped on the gunnel, all set for the quick change when a fish had been caught. The rise of the sedges could go off as unexpectedly as it began. There was no time to lose after a fish had been netted. Off with the messed up fly and on with the fresh one. No team of technicians in a Grand Prix pit stop could change a car wheel as quickly as we could whip on a fresh Green Peter. Still, it is extraordinary how all your fingers will become thumbs when you hear another's reel running out line behind your back with a fish plunging at the end of it.

Above all other forms of angling, fishing with the Green Peter is a cult. 'God's in his heaven/All's right with the world' (Robert Browning). The period of waiting gave time to observe. The trees would never look more verdant, the hills never more majestic, and 'evening all a purple glow' in the words of W.B.Yeats. The solemn nature of the occasion would be enhanced by the ritual silence. Not a sound to be heard except a subdued swish as someone false casted in the still air to take memory kinks out of a dryline. I vividly recall such an evening when a group of anglers from Northern Ireland were waiting in their boats beside me. Now and again a guttural Belfast accent would enquire: 'Ere a stir over your way, Jemmy lad?' The reply: 'Not yet, bit airly.'

Around the headlands the boats waited solemnly at favoured stations as men stood to attention, fervent and expectant as never in Church. Twelve boats in sight, all quietly waiting. Then, from the inner recess of Portloman shore there came a craft somewhat like a motorised bathtub. Its outboard engine put-putted noisily, the driver draped over the stern with three trolling rods fanning out behind. He zigzagged through the silent congregation like a tipsy wino at a funeral. Sacrilege! Outrage! Then came that sharp Belfast growl salted with an expletive: 'Take yon contraption away to hell outa here!' It was, as Damon Runyon would say, enough to make a bishop kick a hole in a stained-glass window.

From Maynooth, Loughs Ennell, Sheelin and Owel were within comfortable range, even for an evening's fishing. Lough Arrow was somewhat further to the north-west. It was a fair distance but its special attraction was in its record of big trout. A friend of ours, Frank Doris, a native of Longford, constantly sang its praises on this front. He was a detective inspector in Dublin Castle and was frequently a welcome fishing partner with us on Lough Ennell. Anyway, he persuaded Brendan Devlin and me to test the mayfly fishing on Lough Arrow. He marked on our card the best places to fish. We would be spoiled for choice but he thought that Ringbawn Bay should have a good fall of spent gnat for evening fishing. I still have his written marks on the Inland Fisheries Trust map to that effect.

Anyway, we did not break his word and on arrival at Arrow struck out across the lake for Ringbawn Bay. What a beautiful location it was, a half moon shape ringed with trees and with promising reed and weed beds. With the spent gnat already dropping we wasted no time admiring the scenery. Brendan soon had one of those famed Lough Arrow trout on the line. I unshipped the oars and moved out to clear water away from the weed and reed beds and various other obstacles. The fish went on a leisurely cruise out the bay. This was not appreciated by a rival angler who had taken up his station some distance ahead. I was concerned about disturbing his water but was not prepared for the barrage of vitriolic language that warned us off his patch.

Anyway, we got the trout. Afterwards, in telling the story to the bold Frank he was highly amused. I had a strong suspicion that he had set us up to trespass on an area where he guessed that our short-tempered permanent tenant would be on location. One can imagine how there was little lost in the telling afterwards. This is what makes for great companionship, having a colourful partner beside one in the boat. Frank was nothing if not colourful. His repertoire of experiences in a lifetime of fishing and shooting, which he shared with his companion John Lynch, would be salted with stories of his activities as a detective.

If I were anywhere near Lough Arrow I would have made a detour for a few hours on the lake, particularly at mayfly time. On one such trip I met up with Bishop Eugene Doherty of Dromore diocese, a mighty man with the fishing rod, well into his eighties. It was blowing hard so we ran for shelter into calmer water in Jack's Bay. He was dapping the natural mayfly while I had the artificial afloat with a large Connemara Black hanging beneath as tail fly. This combination really intrigued him until he realised that the fly floating on the surface ripples was working the wet fly beneath as a nymph. He changed his cast forthwith and claimed that he had one of the best day's angling of his life. When he would come to Maynooth for meetings of the Bishops' Conference he would seek me out to discuss the glory of those hours in Jack's Bay.

He took holidays in the Butler Arms in Waterville with two brother bishops from across the water – Archbishop Murphy of Cardiff and Bishop Ellis of Nottingham. I had met both of them as they fished with him on Lough Arrow. It was Bishop Eugene Doherty who described to me in glowing terms the quality of the sea trout fishing in Lough Currane. I had now set my heart on that, while still allowing for the legitimate exaggeration in a fisherman's recall.

5. The Call of the Sea Trout

In Meelin we first made contact with sea trout in the Feale just beyond Rockchapel. They were there called 'white trout' in contrast to the common brown trout of our local streams. Their name indicated that they migrated from the sea on their way to spawn in the inland headwaters. Before the vast areas of Coillte forestry had been planted, the Feale was a spate river. It rose fast after a downpour in the upland catchment area and dropped back quickly to its normal height. The time to be on the bank was at the first colouring of the flood. In anticipation, in my youthful days, we would have our tin of blueheads at the ready, with the rod tied to the bar of the bike and the Wellingtons astride. At our desks we watched that minute hand on the school clock climbing sluggishly to the hour of three, hoping that Master Brown would not log on extra time. We dared not reveal our impatience because that might just attract the condign response of further injury time.

By the time we got to Thado's Cross the old hands would already have taken up the choice positions. You might buy into their good graces if you had a few select blueheads to spare. You would then learn from them where and how best to present the worms. After years of observation they knew exactly where the shoal of white trout would lodge in the pools at any given height of water and strength of flow. If you had really bought into their goodwill they would advise you on which areas to avoid. We later discovered that various traps, which included a double bed spring, happened to be set permanently in the long reach of calm water which featured below the best fishing in that stretch. No one admitted to placing it there. 'Outsiders Beware' should have been the message if fair play were a consideration.

On the headwaters of the Feale the sea trout were generally around a pound in weight, a far cry from what Waterville was then producing if one were to believe *The Cork Examiner.* Each week it would carry a special column on the catch of salmon and sea trout with a register of names that read like a who's who of Irish gentry and professionals. They would have settled in for weeks at a time in the Butler Arms Hotel. Some passed the whole summer in contented retirement among the angling fraternity. One decided to settle there permanently, somewhat like the old-time German prince-bishop on his way to Rome, who discovered excellent wine in Montefiascone and decided to terminate his journey there and then.

It was many years before I had the opportunity in Waterville of sampling what was evidently on offer for the taking. Bishop Eamonn Casey's ordination class was celebrating their Silver Jubilee at Bettystown, not far from Lough Sheelin, in June 1976. It was there I came to meet Fr Seán O'Leary, who was keen to visit Lough Sheelin with me. In an evening's fishing we produced enough trout to feed the whole jubilee group in his class – much to the dismay of some Dublin clergy, who had been boasting about the superb fishing in Lough Carra where they had caught a few trout the previous week. You can imagine how Seán played them on a long line – as if that last night's bag was just par for the course for a Kerryman.

Seán was not prepared to let it go with the midlands and its relatively short summer season. For him Lough Currane in Waterville reigned supreme and whatever *The Cork Examiner* had proclaimed was no better than the bare truth. He was all set to visit his brother Fr Frank, a Columban priest in Santiago, Chile, but arranged that in the meantime I meet up with Fr Seán O'Keeffe, administrator of the parish of Killarney, who was also well acquainted with the Waterville lakes. It was an angling revelation in every sense of the word. On our first evening on Lough Currane we encountered a shoal of fresh run sea trout averaging over two pounds. As the saying goes, they set the reels on fire. At that time, thirty years ago now, the quality of the sea trout fishing in Waterville would not be credited today. I could expend reams of paper on describing the what, the where and the how at that time, but I am more interested here in the human aspect of the Waterville experience.

Four priests had pooled their resources to purchase an abandoned cottage at Macernane, ideally sited over three of the upper lakes – Lough Eisc-an-Mhactíré (shortened locally to Lough-na-hEisge), Lough Cloonauglin and Lough na Móna. Fr Seán O'Leary, his brothers Eoin and Frank, both Columban priests, and Fr John O'Keeffe were the partners. The property in the mid-1970s was bought for £800! To get some fix on that price one must keep in mind that a VW Beetle then would have come at around £400. There was a verbal codicil in the sale agreement to the effect that the priests would supply a freezer to the vendor. Of course, the subtext there was that the clergy would use their influence to get the Rural Electrification Scheme to extend its service to that isolated area. The female vendor had her priorities right.

The restoration of the Macernane cottage is some saga. The first task towards making the place habitable was to put the shovels to work in clearing out a building where sheep had sheltered from the elements for a generation. Talk about Hercules and the Augean Stables! Then the fitting of doors and windows and lining the roof with a sheet of builders' plastic – a short cut which complicated matters later. All the internal fittings were sourced from contacts who had to hand various items redundant or surplus to their requirements. The *pièce de résistance* was a pitchpine circular staircase salvaged from a convent organ loft. On one occasion a *meitheal* was commissioned to run out a line of plastic piping from the house up to the outfall from Lough-na-mBreac Dearg high across the valley. This was a very technical job in getting the elevation right. If the pressure of the 'head' were too high it would pull apart the connecting joints along the way and in the house. That water supply is still working as planned and still provides a number of spurs off the main line to neighbouring farmers.

Fr Seán had a gift for improvisation from his farming background and his time on mission with the Columbans in Peru. When it came to salvaging and recycling material to new use he was truly gifted. No two radiators would be quite similar in appearance but essentially the system always worked. The overall effect might seem Third World but it served its purpose well. He had a clear picture of what Macernane should be as a welcoming centre for all the friends, anglers or not. He surely was a prince in his house. When anyone lifted the latch his voice would boom, 'Well, look who's here! Come on in!' Then up to the fire and out with the bottle to celebrate the arrival of an unexpected guest. His motto was *'Is túisce deoch ná scéal'* – a welcoming drink before exchange of news.

That large brick kiln-like fireplace was the centre of the house. If *focus* is the Latin term for 'hearth', the word was never more justified than in Macernane. There, a mixture of wood and turf would blaze brightly to throw shadows on the walls and the back boiler would bring those mismatched radiators to boiling point. One sophisticated guest was rather taken aback as he noted a tree trunk being gradually fed from out the floor to keep the fire fuelled. He remarked that Macernane reminded him of Fred Flintstone and family!

That cottage was at the centre of our angling experience for those Waterville sea trout. There plans for the day were laid, weather forecasts were checked and tackle was readied. Later that night results were checked before a blazing fire, while the Dutch oven sizzled and the pressure cooker purred. I was usually voted on to the cooker detail. Food was typically a matter of pot luck. One was better off to be left to work on one's own. The old adage 'Too many cooks ...' definitely added up to good sense on one occasion when a guest offered to assist. The sink stopper went astray, only to be discovered later as an unexpected addition to the Irish stew. The story followed him to his grave.

The menu would vary. Strange as it may now seem, you could have a surfeit of sea trout. Those fresh sea trout would typically have been cooked on a bed of onions in the Dutch oven. There is no better way to preserve quality and flavour. Next in line was a good sized roast chicken, stuffed in the traditional way with bread crumbs, onion, mixed fruit and whatever came the way. What made the big difference were the thick cuts of smoked streaky bacon placed on the chicken once it began to brown. During the long stay in the oven there would be queries from the hungry group around the fireside on whether the chicken would be cooked by Christmas! I doubt that it would feature in Darina Allen's *haute cuisine* menu in famed Ballymaloe, but it was always voted a winner. Nothing like a day on the lake to sharpen an appetite.

The cottage at Macernane is strategically placed. The actual site is exquisite, facing across Lough-na-hEisge to a sheer cliff face which runs cataracts of white water in a spate. Further around to the left you have the run-off from Lough-na-mBreac Dearg, a high mountain tarn which owes its name to the char, a small fish landlocked since the Ice Age in these upper lakes of the Comeragh system. Imagine the atmosphere when the only sound to break the silence is that symphony of cascading waters! In the deep mid-winter there is also a feature which gives the immediate environment an otherworldly feel. From early December until February, the low trajectory of the winter sun runs along just under the rim of the mountain opposite as if a draughtsman had so sketched it. People on first experience sometimes found this perspective unnerving, as if one had been transported into the Land of the Midnight Sun with something like the glow of an Aurora Borealis marking the horizon. They would then appreciate the welcoming warmth of the fire that in winter always blazed inside, full width across the broad hearth.

But then what a transformation of a morning when the spring sun breaks free from the grip of that dark mountain and following the trajectory of that high horizon rolls along the rim hour after hour until the night calls it back at evening. It is then that Macernane, the traditional name of the local area, justifies itself. We had a good neighbour in Paddy Moran, a most lovable man and a mine of information. Brendan Devlin, interested as ever in all things Gaelic, discovered from him that the source of the name was Macha-na-Gréine, which specified the paddock in front of the house as the summer milking area. Well timed the name certainly was because the period for milking coincided with the sun warming and lengthening the days. '*Samhradh, samhradh, bainne na ngamhna, tugaimid féin an samhradh linn.*' That old dancing tune conjured memories of new born calves enjoying the brightness of spring.

Paddy must have been a fine Gaelic speaker in his youth. Now well into his eighties his language in both construction and terminology reflected that tradition. He and I became even closer when all my companions of yesteryear had gone to the Lord and left Macernane a lonely place. Whenever I arrived, Dara, the Red Setter that accompanied me everywhere, would voice his presence to other dogs in the vicinity. Paddy would then step outside his door and check to see whether the smoke was up. Then, stick in hand, he would make his way up to the cottage. I would there celebrate Mass and cook a meal. Then I would produce the bottle of Jameson as we sat around the fire afterwards, recalling old times.

Paddy, like all of his generation, was deeply Christian in his attitude to life. Providence had called on him to resign himself to a series of family tragedies quite out of the ordinary. On one occasion, when Dara had gone through his preliminary barking ritual and with the smoke well up, there was no sign of Paddy. Naturally I was concerned. I went down and quietly lifted the latch to find him on his knees, having dropped off to sleep at the fireside chair with the rosary beads in his hands. I respected his privacy and quietly withdrew. After a while I sent Dara out to repeat his ritual performance of calling all to order and Paddy shortly appeared. A year or so later, on being informed that he was comatose in the hospital at Cahirciveen, I went back straightaway. After praying on my knees beside the bed, I whispered quietly to him, 'Paddy, the smoke is up'. At this he stirred and looked at me with clear recognition. Within an hour or so he passed away. As Scripture would say, 'He was gathered to his fathers'.

So far I have spoken of the magical and emotional quality of the site at Macernane. For Seán O'Leary and Daniel O'Connell, his fishing partner, the location had a major physical advantage, which first attracted their interest through being placed right at the heart of the cluster of upper lakes in the Comeragh system – Lough-na-hEisge, Lough Cloonaughlin and Lough-na-Móna. Lough Derriana required a detour, which it more than justified. In addition to sea trout, Derriana had a good stock of brown trout, well fed and doughty fighters. These upper lakes would also hold salmon, which were sometimes caught on lines trolled behind a boat. That practice of trolling had no attraction for us. Our angling fraternity dismissed it as a crudely mechanical method of fishing. A cast of three wet flies of tried and tested patterns was our standard usage for sea trout. If a salmon or grilse came that way it was surely more than welcome and indeed provided the best of sport on a light trout rod and fine tackle.

Daniel O always claimed that for good fishing it was essential to manouevre the boat. In controlling and directing the boat, or 'fishing the boat', he was a magician. On a drift downwind he would guide the boat with a single paddle out the back on a zig-zag course, a very worthwhile means of covering water in a light breeze. His skill in holding the boat out with strokes of that back paddle while fishing an on-shore wind seemed second nature to him. It looked so easy but it required exquisite balance and timing for each stroke. He boasted that any disciple of his would readily be identified on a lake once he had taken that back paddle in his hand.

Lough-na-hEisge in front of Macernane may seem just a dark deep dour pool. Dark and deep it certainly is, but far from dour. Given the size and closeness of the mountain crowding over it, one tends to underestimate its size. You quickly realise your mistake if you are rowing the boat back into the wind on returning from a drift. Now for the surprise! This relatively small, very deep lake used to hold the finest sea trout in the whole system, running at two to four pounds in weight. Unfortunately, the little stream, which drains the lake, was a ready target for local poachers. Fewer and fewer of those splendid fish succeeded in running the gauntlet up to their spawning grounds in the lake.

With Paddy Moran, who controlled access to the boat, we decided to preserve the lake and improve the spawning grounds at the outlet with the addition of gravel from the large deposit at Bun-na-hEisge at the foot of the ravine across the lake. This was the ideal solution towards making good the loss of material from the outgoing end which constituted the best spawning area. Over the years, the activities of large sea trout in preparing their redds had kicked much of the loose material down the outgoing current. We drew many hundreds of bags of prime gravel by boat from Bunna-hEisge and built up the broad area of spawning beds.

It was an ideal occupation for the calm days of summer. We had the satisfaction of work well done and the further satisfaction later towards year's end of seeing a good number of large sea trout luxuriating in those improved spawning conditions. That was in 1990 and, apart from a few expeditionary test runs, the boat was not availed of for angling. Of course, the poachers also gained in the process both with nets in the outgoing stream and with otterboards trolling flies over the drift along the shore. The otterboard was an ingenious invention. It was a flat board with a diagonal keel strip to direct it out to the side as one drew it alone in the water by the shore. It was a choice weapon for poachers. I am afraid that those poachers sometimes returned to their cars to find them immobilised with a potato stuffed well up the exhaust. Still, one could have lived with poaching to a limited degree at any rate, were it not for the later overall decline in sea trout numbers across the general Waterville system.

Brendan Devlin has retained happy memories of Lough-na-hEisge from his very first experience on the lake. As I rowed the boat at a leisurely pace up to the outlet after sunset on a glorious summer day, I regaled him with the quality of fish he should expect here in contrast to what he had known in the Connemara lakes. He carried a neat nine-foot split cane rod of which he was inordinately proud, even though I had looked askance at it as he threaded on the line. As I squared up the boat for him to start fishing, he made a first tentative cast under the shadow of a holly bush, a favourite lie for large sea trout in hot weather. The result was explosive as the line screamed off the reel right down into the depths. He was fortunate in holding that light rod clear of the gunnel or there would have been a smash. On winding up the line he observed the broken nylon cast and then laid that cane rod carefully in the boat, proposing that I pull back to the house for the loan of a more serviceable fibreglass rod from those lined up on the rafters. Ever afterwards the mention of fishing Lough-na-hEisge brought the hint of a rueful smile.

At the back of the cottage there are twin lakes, Lough-na-Móna and Lough Cloonaughlin. They were both well provided with sea trout right through the year. Of those twin lakes, Cloonaughlin was the more favoured for its rugged environment and greater variety of fishing territory. The best sea trout lies were of course trade secrets. The access point was within a few hundred yards from the cottage. It would be tiresome to record for the reader the scale of our angling experience there. Let us say simply that it generally rated as our first choice amid all the options. For me it carries the poignant memory of having Daniel O with me there on his final angling trip. It was undertaken at his personal request on what I suspect he knew to be his *turas báis*, the final farewell to familiar places by one on the threshold of death. Once he was seated in the boat with the paddles in his hands, he took control as usual in response to my query: 'Well, captain, where to now?' My photograph of him with our last Cloonaughlin trout softens the heart and starts a few tears. We are all familiar with that overused cliché about drawing a line in the sand. Well that is a fair description of the significance for me of that final evening with Daniel O on Cloonaughlin.

Macernane was now to be a dark place in spite of the bright promise in its name. When one parked the car outside the closed door the shadows descended. With growing reluctance I would still visit in memory of old times, particularly while Fr John O'Keeffe was along to accompany me. Once the fire was blazing brightly as ever it dissipated the surrounding shadows. We would offer Mass for our dead companions and for the many friends who would have gathered there to celebrate many a riotous welcome to the New Year in days past.

Old acquaintances will be relieved to know that the cottage at Macernane has been raised like the Phoenix from its ashes. The white knight responsible is a close friend with whom I share an interest in angling and wildlife. Michael Gass met with me under inauspicious circumstances when Daniel O and I had taken his boat out on Cloonaughlin without leave. For someone brought up in English ways this was certainly not cricket. Daniel O, who had a proprietory feel for Cloonaughlin, was reaching for the most withering words in his verbal panoply when I asked him to sit in the car and leave me to talk to the gentleman. I explained that the other boat had broken up on the rocks after someone had set it adrift. We understood one another straightaway to the extent that he joined us around the fire in the cottage and requested that we contact him whenever we needed a boat.

It later emerged that Michael Gass had been as bewitched by the Macernane experience as we had been. He had been a familiar figure in the angling scene in Waterville for close on half a century, when the Butler Arms hotel would have drawn a large contingent of English visitors. His admiring account to us on that first night at Macernane of the stamina and expertise required of the gillies in managing boats on the lakes by oars alone without outboard engines gained him the approval of Daniel O.

Even though Michael Gass had commuted for years between his homes in Cheshire and Waterville, he set his heart on Macernane. With his professional background in the property business he determined that the potential of the site required major reconstruction and upgrading of the now derelict cottage. The financial outlay in the purchase and rebuilding was very substantial, but what has been achieved stands to his credit as someone who envisioned exactly what that unique environment required. The generous hearth with its blazing fire is still the focus as it ever was. When one looks south through the window at those cataracts still flowing down to Bun-na-hEisge, one senses that timeless quality which one rarely experiences in today's fast-forward world.

I number Michael Gass as one of those who puts his cards on the table and, better still, puts his money where his mouth is once he undertakes a task. He has a genuine interest in restoring the sea trout tradition of Waterville. What I appreciate most is that this springs from an overall concern for wildlife and the general ecosphere. I have been delighted to accompany him on occasion to work on improving spawning grounds and clearing feeder streams. This has now become a general concern of the gillies and the loyal anglers who frequent Waterville over the years. That active commitment should help to make the activity of poachers socially unacceptable.

So far in this chapter on the sea trout I have centred attention on Kerry because that has been the major theatre of operations for me. Donegal became a most interesting outreach once I had made the acquaintance of Fr Mark Coyle based at the Capuchin Friary in Árd Mhuire near Creeslough. Again, as in the case of both Seán O'Leary and Michael Gass, the friendship quickly grew from a chance meeting. This happened at a Capuchin conference on moral theology in the early 1970s at their St Bonaventure's Scholasticate in Cork. I have already explained in *Putting Hand to the Plough* how my grandfather's links with the Capuchins had been a factor in my early years. Fr Mark has been everything that I could have envisioned a Capuchin to be.

Once we had come to talk about fishing on that occasion in Cork, we exchanged invitations to Kerry and Donegal. I found myself adopted as a brother by Fr Mark's Donegal angling fraternity and came to feel quite at home through the welcome extended by the friars in Árd Mhuire. Even though the friary was a busy place with summer retreats it had little in common with institutions that typically stand on ceremony. It was an open house and no matter when you returned from the waters and the wild you found your way to the warm kitchen where the large Aga was always on stand-by mode. This atmosphere of welcoming informality has been a characteristic of Capuchin friaries everywhere in the world – and I can vouch for that from wide experience in many lands.

As for angling, Donegal was literally a cornucopia. The sea trout generally might not run as large in size as at Waterville but what a variety of places to fish for them! If you scan a map of Donegal you will note that its northern and western regions are festooned with lakes. They run in strings along feeder rivers where the linked series of lakes would be traditionally described as 'pater nosters' on the pattern of the Our Father beads in the Rosary. Most have ready access to the coast and would carry a good run of sea trout. All will have native lake trout in plenty in pristine waters that are totally free of both domestic and industrial pollution. Of course the glory of Donegal is its rugged scenery. This was a revelation after the flat featureless Westmeath lakes where the mayfly frenzy is the saving grace.

The lake closest to the friary at Ards is Lough Glen. There the sea trout and salmon rest after their short but strenuous ascent up the Lackagh from the sea. There I came to meet Fr Mark's angling fraternity where a fishing hut provided by a Major Neville Chance was the centre of operations. With his dapper gait and moustache he was the very image of a military man straight from the Sandhurst parade ground into action at the front. By then retired from his farm in the Lagan valley, he dedicated quality time to angling. To be with him was a joy. A big occasion was the ritual meal cooked over the fire in the hut to celebrate the arrival of the first new potatoes. The pattern of the menu was sacrosanct. Boiled new potatoes, butter and salt, fresh shallots and a jug of buttermilk. Nothing else was allowed on the table. My best memory of the Major comes from his visit to Waterville. In my mind's eye I still see him draped over the outboard in a halo of pipe smoke as he and Fr Mark launch on to Lough Currane, the very model of an old style fisherman with all the paraphernalia. In his face was that look of contentment that God was in his heaven and all was right with the world. Death when it came held no fear for him. He was a man of absolute integrity in all his dealings. As a deeply committed Catholic he had taken pride in personally driving the Jeep along the front line when the chaplain was on his rounds. Danger carried no fear for him.

Reminiscence tends to run away with me when I recall those Donegal brethren of the angle. Liam Roarty, Peter McCloone, John McIntyre and more recently Eddie Carr and Bishop Seamus Hegarty, then Bishop of Raphoe. The bishop was a late convert to the practice of the angle but, as happens with many converts, he made up for that oversight by total commitment and a competitive spirit second to none. He and Eddie Carr came down to me in Waterville and it was all action with the bishop firm in his intent to be top rod. The German term *schadenfreude* ideally describes my malicious delight in the bishop's discomfiture when Eddie Carr landed a mighty sea trout on Lough Derriana, having played the fish in full view of the opposition.

I could spend a deal of time in providing an account of the features and properties of the various lakes in Donegal with which I became familiar over the years. One lake stands out over all others: Lough Veagh. The story of Glenveagh reaches back to the *drochshaol* of the Famine times with clearances by landlords filling the emigrant ships. Lord Leitrim cleared Glenveagh to make space for a deer park. A successor of the McElhinney family which had been evicted had prospered in America in the construction business. He came back to reclaim their heritage. On his death he donated the property to the state as a public amenity. What a glorious panorama it presents centred on a quite modern but by now well weathered castle nestled into the lake shore. For us the centre of interest was the lake itself. Lough Veagh is a very large body of water situated in a deep valley girded by sheer mountains to left and right. In a north-west wind from the heights of Glendowan it can be a treacherous place if one happens to be caught at any distance from home, granted that the castle boats are very seaworthy in expectation of these conditions.

The great attraction in Lough Veagh is the variety of fish it provides. The sea trout mixed with a fair sprinkling of salmon make the north end of the lake close to the spawning run the main attraction for the angler hoping for the larger fish. The southern part of the lake has more extensive fishing grounds, which hold a good supply of both sea trout and fair-sized lake brown trout. This area is particularly welcome when the wind blows too hard on the main lake, as it often does.

On one unusually calm September day, our group decided to climb the steep mountain behind the castle in the hope that up at the top there would be a breeze on Lough Bradan. The knowledge that a boat had been hauled up to that almost inaccessible location was a fair indication that there must be fish in the lake. The Irish Lough Bradan translates as Salmon Lake, but it would have been quite out of the question for salmon to migrate up there – unless they had swapped their fins for wings! I assume that the lake would have been stocked with trout from some outside source. The surprise was the splendid silvery fish in that same lake. No one identified the source but the quality of those fish may well point to the legendary Lough Leven trout, which were frequently in demand for stocking by the British angling fraternity. It was a most enjoyable day in the heart of an unspoiled terrain. The only sounds that broke the silence were the croaks of the raven and the bellows of the red deer stag in the autumn rut. Lough Bradan is without question the most inaccessible lake of my angling experience, but it has left with me a unique memory of Donegal.

What remained even more with me was the possible link with Scotland's Loch Leven and its native trout of legendary quality. All the old angling authors spoke of fishing in Lough Leven with near religious awe. I had dreamed that one day I would make the pilgrimage. If the trout in that mountain lake in Donegal, where feeding was sparse, gave such sport, one could only wonder what their well-fed cousins would be like in their original rich habitat.

The opportunity came when a niece in Dundee asked me to celebrate her marriage. Fond indeed I was of that niece but Dundee rang more than wedding bells. It is situated within a short distance of Kinross, the main point of access to Loch Leven. My palm itched for the feel of the butt of a fly rod bent double in a specimen or near specimen of those famed trout. Ned Crimmins, that niece's father, now sadly deceased, was not an angler but he was keen to share the adventure. My excitement was infectious. It was already decided that any trout caught would be released back into the lake after he had taken the photographs as record for posterity. Anyway, to knock on the head with the 'priest' one of those legendary trout would have been close to sacrilege.

The large circle of moored boats at the wharf on Kinross pier was certainly impressive. On closer inspection both boats and outboard engines seemed somewhat vintage.

Worse was the total absence of anglers and the lack of the kind of atmosphere one associates with a group gearing up for a day's fishing. What a day it was; mixed cloud and sun, a nice wave on the lake. Conditions ideal but ne'er a boat out on the water.

So far I was surprised, but the shock was to come when we followed the sign to the office identified as Headquarters of Scotland's Fisheries Board. We were welcomed by a well-informed official who told us the story. Loch Leven of those famed trout was no more. The lake had now been stocked with rainbows but even for them the fishing was very slow. He read my shocked expression and expressed his sympathy. When I got back to Ireland I approached some knowledgeable friends. Michael Gass shared the grief and expressed his regret that I had not spoken with him before I launched on my odyssey to the Promised Land. The pristine loughs in Scotland further north were where the angling for both native and migratory fish was still of that legendary quality. Dermot Linehan, whose sons Michael and James are international anglers, told me that Loch Leven had been de-registered from the list of championship venues. It was the death of a life-long dream. I returned home more than resigned to what Irish lakes have to offer.

6. The Salmon King of Lake and River

In my early years in Meelin, angling was confined to fishing for brown trout, which were then plentiful in the Dallow and Allow, feeder streams of the Blackwater. We knew of course that in the closed season, once autumn had turned into winter, these same streams, as well as the smaller tributaries, were where salmon came to spawn. This left the fish vulnerable as they excavated and prepared the redds on the shallow gravel spawning beds, in which they would deposit and fertilize the eggs that would generate the next generation. Some enterprising locals would then turn poachers and stalk the rivers with home-made gaffs and tridents to ambush the spawning fish. This was done at night with a sod of turf generally soaked in tvo (Tractor Vapourising Oil) to target fish that had taken up position on the shallows. The flesh of spawning fish would have been tasteless and not good for the table, but in hard times it must have been acceptable.

By our days it was the sense of adventure that really counted, at a time when there was little enough variety in life for active young men over winter. Here also the hunter-gatherer instinct of our prehistoric ancestors had an oppor-tunity to express itself in an adventurous setting. Often in the dark of the night, as we traveled along a country road, my father might spot the flickering light down on the riverbank and would comment that the boys were on the move tonight. Close to Meelin, a favourite spawning location was the Abha-an-Áir stream, which had many gravel beds and was quite accessible from a winding road that followed its course for a mile or so. This accessibility would have also exposed it to the attention of the local Garda, which in Meelin to our knowledge was more notional than actual. In other places it would have provided a trial of wit between poacher and policeman where old scores might be settled. On occasion, an overactive Garda might open his door in the morning to find a salmon's head tied to the knocker with the question, 'Where were you when I was killed last night?'

That note of rivalry would have added a frisson of risk to the practice of poaching. There were indeed very real dangers as well. TVO, paraffin and diesel might not be at hand to fuel the lighted sod of turf and petrol would be substituted. That was highly volatile and any careless handling during the lighting process could have serious consequences. One local was fortunate to escape injury to his face when the highly flammable petrol flared as he lit the sod. He lost all the hair from the front of his scalp. The neighbours enjoyed his predicament as he was compelled to wear a cap to conceal the damage. He would come late to Mass and remain in the porch with cap on, ready to bolt as the priest left the altar. Poaching in the Meelin area came to a tragic end when a young man lost his life, having stumbled in the dark into a deep pool where he became trapped in a submerged tree.

Before I ever saw a salmon in its natural element I had read everything about them in whatever books I could lay hands on, particularly in those bequeathed by priest anglers to the general reading library at St Colman's College in Fermoy. It was pure magic. This wonderful fish had begun

life as tiny fry off the spawning bed, then developed
through the stages of parr and smolt until it migrated to
the sea. It would have been a perilous life journey to get far
out and up to the rich feeding grounds around Greenland
with so many predators waiting along the way. Only a very
small fraction of smolts would make it to those feeding
grounds.

When later the spawning instinct hinted that it was time
to return to its original home, this is just what the salmon
did, precisely on course over a vast distance at sea to the
very stream in which its life had begun. Here was a mystery
indeed. How did it steer this course? It must have preserved
some innate memory of the water environment through
which it had threaded its way as a little smolt a year or so
ago. On the return journey it would have had more obstacles
to face. Killer whales and seals would patrol the currents,
nets would be set in waiting, anglers would ply their
expertise, waterfalls would have to be surmounted. Instinct
would drive it forward, all obstacles to the contrary not-
withstanding. What a tragedy that the poacher's gaff should
end the story just as the mature salmon had made it home,
ready to start the cycle again where it had been hatched.

All that story had remained a dream until I met with Jim
and Rosalie O'Callaghan, a Dublin family which had a
salmon fishery on the Feale at Kilmorna. Their beautiful
cottage, named Bárr-na-Féile, was right over one of the
finest salmon pools on the Feale. The Cot Pool was an ideal
holding stopover for salmon running through from the
Cashen estuary. A generation ago, when I came to know
that part of the Feale, it was well on the way to being
reduced to a shadow of its earlier phase when large numbers of spring salmon would have rested there. Fish of up
to twenty pounds were frequently recorded. Tom Dillon,

the farmer from whom the O'Callaghans had acquired the fishery, would recount what a bonanza the Feale would have provided when those spring fish were on the move.

The first time I saw a salmon hooked and landed was in the Cot Pool by Jim O'Callaghan. It was a fresh run fish of over ten pounds. The concept of the salmon as king of the river was well justified on this occasion. That fresh run fish, once on the line, spent as much time in the air as in the water, leaping and whirling all over the pool. I had seen sea trout perform with similar energy on a smaller scale but this was an amazing show of power. Jim as an experienced angler knew when to hold and when to ease on the line. Eventually he beached the fish at the tail of the pool where I stood ready with the net, if and when needed. He taught me that I should hold off with the net until one had the salmon's head exposed on the surface of the water. Then either he would slide the fish over the net or I would slide the net under the fish. The last thing one should do was snatch at the fish with net or gaff and risk fouling the line.

So I had my first sight of a salmon being played on a rod and my first lesson on how to land a salmon. I had a lot to learn about fishing for salmon but I had the benefit of good mentors in Jim O'Callaghan and Tom Dillon.

Tom Dillon was a specialist in fishing with the worm. Fly fishing for salmon in the Cot Pool was not productive, but fishing with the artificial lure might bring good results on occasion. The choice above everything else was the blue-head worm, of which Tom had a cache in ideal conditions in the debris at the back of his hay barn. From there we too were kept well supplied. Tom was an expert in trotting the worm down the pool at different depths in the current to where he knew salmon were likely to lie in any depth of water. He is now well into his eighties and has always been a gentleman on and off the river. Expert with that bluehead worm he certainly was, but he was generous in sharing that knowledge. When fishing with him, he was at his happiest when one of us got the fish. I can assure you that this is an exceptional trait among anglers at large.

Across the Feale was another farmer, Micheál O'Connor, who would also know when conditions on the river were most likely to have salmon on the move. Salmon, particularly once they have lodged in a pool for a while, tend to be very dour. The problem is that they have no urge to feed once they enter fresh water on their spawning run. They will mouth a worm on occasion but the reason why they go for an artificial lure may be curiosity, aggression or just when in the mood.

I recall one particular March morning, shortly after the season had opened, when Jim O'Callaghan and I were set to go into Listowel. Micheál, on the opposite band of the river, called out that a spate flood was on the way and that we should get back quickly. That we certainly did but what a sight we encountered! On the sparse grass of the far bank were laid out four gleaming fresh salmon with Micheál struggling to land the fifth. Struggle it certainly was with Micheál more like an acrobat than an angler as he played the salmon while standing on the back of one of those submerged cars, which had been placed there to protect the clay bank from erosion by the current. What made the picture really memorable was that the salmon had got in through one of the car's side windows! Micheál had one foot extended down into the water while using the heel of the Wellington to keep the line from contact with the car chassis – meanwhile undoubtedly praying that the fish would return by the same window through which it had gained entry. With the river now in full spate we could do nothing to help. Amazingly he succeeded in landing that fish. In triumph he held up the three-inch Blue Devon lure, which I had slung across to him that morning on his judgement that this would do the business.

Micheál was a born storyteller with a vast amount of local lore on which to draw. I unwittingly provided him with superb material to galvanise the interest of the O'Callaghan family when I reported my experience on a night of wind and rain. I awoke, pulled on the waterproofs and went out to check that the windows of the cars were closed. On the return I heard this eerie wail rising and dying out on the wind. At breakfast I told the children that I had heard the banshee. The disbelief was later replaced with amazement once Micheál had been told the story. Having discovered from Rosalie O'Callaghan that my mother was a Sheehy, he confirmed that a Sheehy could have been related to the Fitzmaurices from Failldearg down the river, one of whom had died in London that same night.

I think that it was the same Micheál who named the O'Callaghan fishing lodge 'Bárr-na-Féile', with that dual meaning of a location above the Feale and a hospitable open house. That has left many happy memories over and above the actual fishing for salmon and sea trout. The kinship bond with the family has been a lifelong experience.

Jim O'Callaghan, an architect/builder by profession, had undertaken the development of a site in Limerick, close to Castleconnell where the salmon fishing was world famous. He leased the five beats in their sequence from the ESB. The Shannon was still a lordly river, even after it had been harnessed at Ardnacrusha for the generation of electricity. It was on Beat 3 that I hooked my first salmon on a fly. That was indeed an experience. I would not have landed it if another angler had not come along in time to provide the net. After that the worm and bait fishing had little attraction. Hefting a fourteen-foot fly rod might test back muscles that one never knew one had. One made light of it in the expectation that a salmon was there for the catching.

Through Jim and Rosalie I came to know Johnny Enright, the last of the internationally known family of Castleconnell rod makers. I spent many happy hours with him in the workshop where his skill in building and balancing split cane salmon rods was now second nature. The modern carbon fibre rods had not yet come into use. My sense is that Johnny would not have been inspired by the uniform factory blanks which compose these rods. The name and fame of the Enrights had been built on the Castleconnell greenheart salmon rods. Greenheart, a costly hardwood, has ever been the choice for quayside bollards and lock gates, where the process of constant drying and wetting would rot other woods in a relatively short time. At first sight this seems a very dead material for fashioning fishing rods, but it had hidden qualities that were treasured by anglers. For rodmaking it was essential to visit the timber yard oneself, where the baulks of wood were available in sixteen-foot lengths. In that dense dark timber it was difficult to identify a fair grain right through to full length. The rodmaker himself could only make that judgement. This was of the very essence of the choice material for a fishing rod. Otherwise, with a false grain the rod would splinter even in the casting.

To demonstrate the quality, Johnny took down an ancient Castleconnell greenheart three-piece salmon rod from the rafters. What an amazing craft had shaped, balanced and refined it from a length of raw wood taken from a Limerick timber yard! The three pieces were joined together by splicing rather than by fixing with ferrules. Johnny explained that the pliable splice made for a fair run of grain right through the bend, rather than the distortion at the ferrule. This was a full-length, sixteen-foot rod for use when the Shannon was once at its untamed natural flow before the ESB dam was built at Ardnacrushe. Compared with today's rods, well balanced as it was, it must have taken powerful casting skills. Johnny as a child had seen his father in action with such a rod, but he respected the antique too much to risk it now. I did see Johnny casting with the fourteen-foot split cane rod. The manner in which he would roll out line and cast to full distance towards the far bank of the Shannon was, if you forgive the cliché, poetry in action. He was slight of build but the rod was like a magic wand that achieved the desired result as if a natural extension of the shoulder and wrist. Johnny suffered severely from haemophilia. Rosalie was in a position to source for him the best treatment recommended at the time, but unfortunately he died at quite a young age.

I have many good memories of the Shannon. Beat 5 was more like a lake than a river. It was there that Jim hooked a monster salmon. After head and tail showing us its size, it took the line over its shoulder and cruised away solidly towards the Clare coast. I ran to get the boat out on Jim's shout that his reel was running on the backing. Run it did to the very end and that was that. The boat was one of the last of the Shannon cots. Driven by a single paddle from the stern like an Indian dug-out canoe, it was flat-bottomed and of shallow draught so that the gillie could hold it in the current for the angler to fish. Jim, for old time's sake, had a cot made for the Feale. I think that the only use of it was by me to give the O'Callaghan youngsters runs on the river. I was given a pair of spare paddles as a souvenir of the one that got away on Beat 5.

After the Feale and the Shannon, any salmon that came the way for me was caught on a light rod in the course of sea trout fishing. Here is where Donegal really scored. The jewel in the crown was the pool at Ramelton. There sea trout and salmon moved in and out on the tide. The salmon fishing was at its best early in the year. This is when Major Neville Chance had access to the fishery. He recalled that he often fished there in January with the freezing line forming ice collars on the agate rings of the salmon rod. I was never on site for the run of spring fish, but later in summer I had a few grilse out of the lower part of the pool. The challenge here was to get below the hooked fish before it made off down for the sea. The secret in salmon fishing is to know that the fish will move against the direction of strong pressure exerted by the angler. One old expert in the craft would say that it was like tethering a pig by the front leg to get it to market. I have never checked this out but he claimed that whatever chance you had of leaving the pig drive itself in front by putting on pressure, you had none whatever of driving it forward yourself!

I have spoken already of the sea trout fishing on Lough Veagh when salmon would also gather in the top bay in anticipation of the spawning run. Fr Mark Coyle had good fortune there on one occasion when he deftly handled a few fish who made every effort to take refuge in a large weed bed close to shore. That same day I will never forget because midges and clegs were on the rampage. The Glenveagh midges were legendary. One native remarked in a farmer's metaphor that it was not so much what they eat as what they trample! The same man said that a Glenveagh man is always known on the streets of Letterkenny because of his conditioned reflex of waving his hands around his head as if he were swatting midges. Strangely enough,

Fr Mark playing salmon was not nearly as conscious of the pests as I, who was managing the boat on station.

I made up for that torturing day on Glenveagh by an extraordinary experience on Glen Lake, best known for its sea trout. This was the first resting place for fish before they ascended the Owencarrow to Lough Veagh, but here salmon were not very partial to take the fly. Whatever changed the mood of those lodgers on a particular day will never be known. Liam Roarty and I were drifting in between the cliffs to the top bay when I hooked a salmon. Without a salmon net and with nowhere to beach it, Liam got on the oars to row back to the hut with the fish in tow. This may seem incredible, but it is well known that on a slow steady draw a salmon will follow quietly. A Gallagher neighbour was sitting in the sun at the hut. He reached out to us with the net. He later spread the story that a monster salmon had towed the boat right across Glen Lake and that it was good fortune that he was there at the hut with the net! There you have another good example of how fishy stories develop, given any grain of truth.

From the few examples which I have provided, you will appreciate that drama of one kind or another is part and parcel of salmon fishing. All freshwater fish are unpredictable, none more so than the salmon. I could multiply those examples – Fr Mark and I dozing in the boat in a dead calm on Waterville's Lough Currane when a salmon swam up lazily and hooked himself on a hanging fly; Frank Doris landing four salmon at Castleconnell in an area on Beat 5 where salmon never featured before; an angler at Feale Bridge near Abbeyfeale discussing how miserable the fishing was as he flicked a cigarette butt into the river to have a salmon rise and take it.

My final acquaintance with the salmon on the Shannon was when that fatal fungus disease hit Ireland in the 1970s. It was a depressing experience to watch those lordly fish circling in the backwaters doomed to die a lingering death. Nothing could be done about it except to wait and pray in hope that it would pass. Thank God, that indeed it did. The finest fish in the whole of creation had survived this natural disaster. It depends on us to secure the future against human destructiveness.

7. The Characters You Meet ～✕

Going up in a lift early of a morning in the County Hall in Cork, I bade the time of day to the only other occupant, who seemed somewhat out of sorts. My simple salutation drew the sour response: 'Nothing wrong with the day. It's just the characters one meets'. That gave me the title for this chapter. Naturally one runs in to a lot of characters in the course of life, but here I centre attention on those who became close friends in the angling scene. True enough, the angling fraternity has its quota of impatient, short-tempered people, but you let them sail by and give them a wide berth. In any case, they rate as a minority in my experience.

Many anglers who are not at all loners in normal life appreciate the sport as an opportunity for quiet reflection. Whether on the riverbank or on the lake angling it serves their purpose ideally. Of its nature, fishing on a river tends to be a rather solitary occupation. In a boat I find companionship a major bonus. If the fishing is slow you exchange anecdotes and call attention to anything unusual in the general scene around. If things are not looking up after an hour or so you weigh up the options. In desperation one colleague of mine would typically suggest that it called for a change of flies 'from the shirt out'. There would be little enough comment on a fish successfully landed in the boat. It was the one that got away that would provide material for analysis of the why and the wherefore – and the fish grew in size in the process.

Among the many I count as close friends on the broad perspective a few would be fishing companions as well, where the angling factor is but one aspect of lifelong friendship. In that context I rate particularly that colleague dating back to our days together on the Maynooth staff. Fr Brendan Devlin and I early made the acquaintance of the great Midland Lakes – Ennell, Sheelin and Owel. There we fished with Fr Mattie Coleman and Oliver Buckley of Mullingar. We became close friends with them but one would hardly describe them as 'characters'. With them everything was well planned and organised so that the unpredictable, which brings out the quality in a 'character', did not generally occur. When I come to describe those whom I designate 'characters' the unpredictable was what switched on the colour in their personalities. I would go so far as to say that something about them courted the unpredictable.

Brendan Devlin would surely agree with me that at the head of the list of 'characters' we should place Fr Seán O'Leary and Daniel O'Connell. I have already described above the circumstances in which I came to meet Seán O'Leary. That led on inevitably to Daniel O because the twain were twins. In their company there was never a dull moment. It is no exaggeration to say that they rarely agreed upfront about anything in fishing or about any problem to be solved in the DIY business. After debating the pros and cons around the options, a working consensus would emerge. If the results did not measure up to expectations no quarter was given in apportioning blame. In the restoring and maintaining of the cottage in Macernane their good-humoured banter made light of the labour. It was in that context that I first came to know them as characters in the true sense of that term. While each brought out the colour in the other they were also characters in their own right. I now wish to focus on this, although it is somewhat like an exercise in separating Siamese twins where the personalities are conjoined.

To all and sundry far and wide Seán O'Leary was known familiarly as 'Father Seán'. Many priests carry that Christian name, but it came to identify him above all others. Many priests were acquainted with a wider public in superficial media terms but few counted so many personal friends and few were known or loved so intimately. That beautiful picture of the Irish priest inspired by the phrase *Saggarth Aroon* fitted him better than anyone I have known. He was a father figure to his family and circle of friends and to all in the parishes where he served as a priest. These parishes stretched from El Porvenir in Peru into the very heart of Kerry, the Black Valley itself.

At his funeral, the late Bishop Michael Murphy of Cork paid him generous tribute for his pioneering work with the Cork Mission to Peru. To his work at home the people of Kerry bore witness when they gathered in thousands to pay him a sad farewell in Cahirciveen in 1993. They were not just thanking him for the buildings he left behind him everywhere he went. They were thanking him as one thanks someone for being one's father or one's brother. Their evident personal grief at his death spoke of that.

If I were asked to name one particular feature that characterised Father Seán's personality, I would propose his capacity to inspire and maintain personal friendship. It was not something he studied – it was spontaneous. He did not court familiarity and popularity, nor did he seek out the rich and famous. He took people as he found them and where he found sincerity there was a friend for life. It did not matter who or what you were. Small and great were all the one to him. His loyalty to his friends was proverbial. A parishioner speaking from personal experience tearfully remarked at his funeral that he would give everything he had and go through fire and water to help you.

An old saying speaks of a generous host as a prince in his house. It well describes Father Seán. He literally ran an open house. He was more than big in height. He had a great heart. His welcome would ring out: 'Well, look who's here. Come on in'. He loved to have a crowd celebrating something or other. Anything was an excuse – a barbecue for the New Year in O'Donoghue's Castle in Glenflesk, a gathering to bring home the turf or whatever. He was in his element once there was action. The Irish term *tiomáint* hits it off well.

He had that luminous quality which marks a great human being. Once he came into a room he set the atmosphere alive and warm. The awkward and the timid were drawn into conversation. The stranger felt at home when he poked fun at someone, as he often did. It was always at someone who could take it and his infectious laugh took all the harm out of it.

He had an endless fund of stories based on true happenings for which he would give chapter and verse. He prized such real incidents away above any made-up yarns. His narrating of the case of the sunburnt sow, which dated back half a century to our so-called Economic War, was his *pièce de résistance*. The sow in question had been trussed, spancelled and laid in the bottom of a boat for transport through the Upper Lake in Killarney and up the Long Reach into the Black Valley. As the hot summer sun toasted her hide she sprang and plunged, overturning the boat and, in the process, dumping herself and the two dozing oarsmen unceremoniously into the water. The elder of the two lads grabbed the drowning pig by the *cluas* (Father Seán's word, more sonorous than ear!) and struck out with a back-stroke for a neighbouring island, leaving his brother to fend for himself. Whatever about that brother's fate, the sow had to be rescued or there would be hell to pay from the father!

As an encore he would tell some of the sayings and adventures of Jim Tangney of Black Valley fame. A would-be client doubtfully surveying one of Jim's boats, patched with tar-soaked strips of *The Kerryman*, queried: 'I say, have you ever lost anyone on the lake?' To which Jim replied: 'Yerra no. We drowned a few all right, but we found them all'. This would be followed by his account of Jim's effort to calm the fears of an anxious passenger who noted a lot of bilge-water in the boat: 'Yerra, that's nothing man, I always keep a drop handy in case of fire'.

Seán was a close observer of nature. His account of the epic battle between pairs of ravens and peregrine falcons disputing a nesting site on O'Donoghue's castle in Glenflesk is unforgettable. The peregrines are made for agility in attack but the ravens are doughty fighters in defence. The falcons ruled the skies but the ravens stoutly held the fort with beaks ready for a lethal stab at the attack-ers. Under unrelenting attack from different directions, the ravens called in reinforcements which had little stomach for the fight. Eventually the ravens called it a day and moved out to seek another option for nesting.

His anecdotes about fishing escapades are memorable, and they were told with typical colourful expressions. Two stories concerned a missionary priest friend who would accompany him while angling on the Laune. On one occa-sion, Seán climbed an oak tree overhanging a pool where a salmon had been rising. It was the best way to get into range for a cast with the bait rod. As he released the bait, the branch on which he was standing gave way. *'Mo léir,'* he

Dara reading my thoughts.

Fr Seán, Daniel O and friends in 1976 with Macernane in the background.

A *meitheal* in the bog at Macernane.

Fr Seán's last outing in Killarney.

Daniel O ready for the action on Lough Currane.

Loch Leven: A dream that did not come true.

Michael Gass in the new Macernane.

Waterville: The angler's farewell prayer.

Another Waterville specimen: sea trout.

Loch Currane: A promising day.

End of year barbeque in Killarney.

Killarney: To the waters and the wild.

said, 'I cleared O'Sullivan into the pool ahead of me'. His unfortunate companion had stretched himself out to get a better view of the action.

On another occasion, fishing the river into a dog-leg pool he hooked a salmon. Out of sight around the corner his priest friend was snoozing when the shout for the net woke him. Disorientated, as he turned around he rolled into the pool and held on to a trailing branch as he called out for rescue. After Seán had beached the fish he came around to be told: 'You are some friend, leaving me to drown while you played that fish!' To which Seán replied: 'I knew you were fine while I heard you calling out. If you had gone silent I would have come around immediately'.

One story would lead to another and he had the way of telling them. All too often prolific talkers tend to be hurlers on the ditch given to *búileam sciath*, shouting encouragement. Father Seán was a doer who loved a challenge, the bigger the better. He was a born leader, always at the hub of the action.

We often said that he had been born out of due time by some four centuries! He would have been quite at home with the likes of O'Sullivan Beare in that epic march from Castletownbere to Breffni O'Rourke in Leitrim after the battle of Kinsale. He had also something of Robinson Crusoe in his make-up. He could improvise in any situation. His Peru experience stood him well here. If something were to be put right in plumbing or electricity or whatever, he would dig out just what was needed from the mixture of handy bits and pieces in the back of his vw van. Where Crusoe turned just one man Friday to work, Father Seán would have press-ganged a *meitheal*. No one could refuse because he worked harder than anyone.

I recall an incident when we were hard at work in mixing aggregate and laying blocks to construct a garage in

Macernane. Along came a dentist friend of Seán who readily fell to work with the shovel in mixing sand and cement,
hard labour if ever there was. Some weeks later Seán met
with the dentist and told him, tongue-in-cheek, that he
was gathering a *meitheal* for further work on the house. The
invitation drew the response: 'No way! After the last
experience my wrists froze up so that I couldn't pull a tooth
for two days!' Seán's enjoyment may be imagined.

That Robinson Crusoe parallel is particularly true in
regard to that derelict cottage which we made habitable at
Macernane. It's the house that Seán built. Everything in it
bears the stamp of his enterprise – the rafters from a cedar
tree cut down in site clearing operations, the circular staircase made redundant from a convent organ loft, the assort-
ment of used radiators surplus to the requirements of
handyman friends, the brick kiln-like fireplace in which you
could roast a bullock. That house was the centre of the
great love of his leisure time: fishing for sea trout. Here
plans were laid, weather forecasts were checked and gear
was readied. Daniel O would have been on site to add colour
to the goings-on. After Seán's death, Daniel O was a lost
soul.

As autumn shaded into winter in 1998, we laid Daniel O
to rest on the heights of Aghadoe, looking down across the
expanse of Lough Lein and the golf course at Mahoney's
Point. It was a fitting place. That Killarney scene had been
background to Daniel O's long life in which fishing and golf
had played so central a part. The turnout of angler and
golfer friends at his funeral came as no surprise. He was the
heart of their world for fifty years.

In any reckoning, Daniel O was an extraordinary man.
Born in 1916, he had spent just three years at the national
school in Lissivigeen when gangrene in a fractured leg

interrupted his formal schooling. His natural intelligence more than made up for that deficit. He was educated at the university of life across a broad sweep of experience in many fields. From an early age he was busy felling and jointing oak for making railway wagons at 7/6 per tree; cutting timber for firewood at 5/- per butt load; breaking stones for the road at 3/- per cubic yard; house-building when the opportunity offered; rowing tourist boats across the lake; gillying in between times. You name it and Daniel O did it. The skills learned in the process, along with his strong personality, marked him down as a natural leader in any enterprise. No wonder Fr Seán and Daniel O struck sparks off one another, like flint and steel.

At the age of forty he joined the ESB as a chargehand linesman. His colleagues tell that nothing was too tough for Daniel O. Whatever had to be done he did it, rain or shine. Over his twenty-five years on the job he made many friends. After his retirement he never missed an ESB outing, even when the fishing was at its best. My association with Daniel O began in 1976 through Fr Seán O'Leary. From that time Daniel O and a trio of us priests, including Dean John O'Keeffe, then parish priest of Tralee, were inseparable. The centre of operations was generally Fr Seán's house at Macernane in Waterville. Anyone who has visited it will never forget the atmosphere of that little house. Fr Seán and Daniel O were principals in its restoration, with bits and pieces gathered from sundry sources. Both were equally skilled at DIY work but frequently, and stridently, differed on how something should be put to rights. Third parties were well advised to keep out of the way as they warmed to the debate hammer and tongs. A battle of Titan and Centaur.

Where fishing was concerned, Daniel O's expertise was unquestioned, although he allowed that on some fronts the master was at risk of being passed out by his pupils. However, this was a smokescreen to put us off our guard and give him an edge in the competition. Daniel O was nothing if not competitive, be it in regard to fish, golf, cards or whatever. As a youngster with his father he had fished the Flesk with worms and woodbees. Then he graduated to the Killarney Lakes. In his eyes, nothing anywhere could compare with them. When pollution and algae closed the fishing there he was devastated. He knew every shoal and corner of those lakes: the Honeycombs, the Half Moon, the Hen and Chickens, Darby's Garden, Robin's Flat, the Heron Rocks. With his characteristic short strokes of the back paddle he guided a boat in and out over those special spots. They were all as familiar to him as the lines on the palm of his hand.

He would have read the conditions and decided where the fish should rise on the day. He was rarely disappointed. That unerring gift of his was uncanny. In these days of genetic engineering one could imagine that a fish gene had been somehow programmed into his brain. He simply had an instinct, a sixth sense. When it came to assessing the results of a day's fishing the evidence was for all to see. Daniel O had no need to exaggerate.

Imagine an angler coming in after a morning out on the lake with three salmon weighing around nine pounds each and three trout of ten, eleven and fourteen pounds all caught in the one area! That was on 11 April, 1983. Even Daniel O, who had a theory for everything, could not explain why these great fish all became suicidal at the one time and in the one place. He wasn't all that jubilant because the fish had fallen to the troll, not to the fly. For him fishing with flies was an art; trolling baits was just work.

He was particularly gifted at tying flies. One watched in amazement as he dressed his famed Hawthorn or Duckfly on a tiny size twelve or fourteen hook. This he continued to do even when his fingers were knarled with arthritis. He had a keen eye for a killer fly. Many an angler had cause to rue the day that gave Daniel O access to a fly box. Fr Mark, a Capuchin friend whose special flies were tied by a soldier on service in the Lebanon, was plucked clean on many occasions. The choice flies would be rolled under the thumb to end up in the cup of the palm. Fr Seán called it the 'Pelican Touch'.

He took great pride in his own fly tying talents. When challenged by Fr Seán on being asleep by the fire when he should have been tying flies for the evening rise, he claimed that he had tied a half-dozen, even though only three were on display beside him. Straight away he put the blame on a marauding spider which had made off with the others.

When Fr John O'Keefe brought back some flamingo feathers from a trip to Kenya, Daniel O tied a pattern which he christened the Fandango. He had words for everything. An English entomologist on the shore of Lough Currane in Waterville showed him an insect like a tiny scorpion and asked for its local name. We had always known it as the Devil's Coachman. Daniel O immediately said that it was the 'Crackerjackjohansson'. You should have seen the roguish glint in his eye as the specialist wrote the manufactured name solemnly into his register. My conscience intervened to say that it was more correctly known as The Devil's Coachman.

Daniel O was certainly a rogue, often setting someone up, but always someone who needed to be brought down a peg for his own and everyone's good. To the one who was down he was the soul of generosity. He detested any hint of malicious gossip. He never wanted to see or leave anyone in trouble where he could help. He was gifted in improvising.

A light went out of Daniel O's life with the unexpected death of Fr Seán O'Leary in July 1993. They had been twin spirits who had shared friendship and companionship for over thirty years. That death put a special duty on we who remained to continue where Fr Seán had left off. The house in Macernane had been preserved just as he left it. A month before he died, Daniel O asked me to take him down for a final visit to say goodbye to the old friends and the old haunts. He was a shadow of his former self but the recall was bright as ever. He knew it was his last visit. In Kerry Irish it would be known as *turas báis*.

He now rests in Aghadoe looking down on his much loved Killarney lake and golf course. He lies beside his wife of fifty years, Margaret, always known as Sis. Theirs surely was a marriage made in heaven. She was up to all his roguery. When he returned to base she would remark that the fishing must have been very bad now that he thought of his wife alone at home! Where he and Sis were concerned, nothing was lost from Eric Cross' book *The Tailor and Ansty*.

We were all better for knowing Fr Seán and Daniel O. What Tomas O'Criomthain of the Blasket Islands said of his fellows we say of them: *'Ní bhfeidh a leithéidí ann arís'*. We will not see their likes again. May the Lord grant them the light of heaven. On the way they may well have exchanged a word or two with St Peter on matters of mutual interest. May they be there to welcome us when our time comes. *I liontaibh Dé go gcastar sinn go léir*. Our hope is that God's net will gather us all into his Kingdom.

Seán O'Leary and Daniel O were at the core of a circle of angling friends. The Linehan family from Cork were in that circle from the beginning. Dermot and his four sons were all committed anglers. I still meet them regularly and we have kept the memories alive. No matter what the fishing was like on the particular day, the gathering for lunch on the lakeside was the highlight. The O'Connells, the Linehans and the rest of us would make it a major celebration in some sheltered mooring corner. No shortage of wood there to fuel the fire blazing under the long-handled frying pans, with a selection of meat and pudding on a bed of onions sizzling in fat. It was not a place for anyone with a sensitive digestive system. A cast iron stomach would not have gone amiss when sharing in that mixed grill. Whatever about the food it was the company that really counted.

I introduced my two friends from Donegal, Fr Mark Coyle from the Capuchin friary in Ards and Bishop Seamus Hegarty of the Diocese of Raphoe. They fitted in immediately and added to the camaraderie on the lake and around the homely fire in Macernane. Whenever we meet now their faces light up with the memory of the doings and sayings. When the bishop had transferred to Derry at a time of turmoil in Northern Ireland, one can imagine what a relief it must have been to pack the fishing rod and take off south for a break. From my experience of being with them in Donegal, the choice of fishing there would have matched anything in the South. However, they admitted that the exchanges between Seán O'Leary and Daniel O made Waterville a special place.

One incident we will never forget was a day of thunder with hailstone squalls that lashed the neighbouring upper lakes of Lough-na-Móna and Lough Cloonaughlin. It was very unusual weather for August. Bishop Seamus was with me on Lough-na-Móna and was of a mind to get to shore. Assuring him that a hailstone squall could get some sluggish fish moving we continued. He hooked and landed a salmon of around ten pounds. Lacking a large net we towed him ashore and beached him.

In his glee I reminded him that Fr Mark and Brendan Devlin would have had similar weather conditions on the other lake. It would be horror if they trumped us. When we reached home we put the salmon out of sight in a fish box, keeping a few sea trout on display. Our friends arrived with contentment written all over them as they produced a prize sea trout. Naturally we were critical of its general quality and appearance, the bishop commenting that it could do with a face lift and a nose job. They regarded this as sour grapes. On my suggestion to put it aside in the fish box, their jaws dropped when they opened it to find that fine salmon. Graciously they conceded defeat.

Regarding that circle of friends, I need to add Dara to complete the picture. Dara, a red setter of extraordinary character, always had his place in the boat. Fr Seán and Daniel O would not launch on the lake without him. That dog seemed to be convinced that the standard ritual he performed guaranteed results. Sitting up on the prow of the boat, he signaled his demand that the first port of call on Lough Currane be the island at the mouth of the Inny River on which a puck goat had been marooned. This poor animal was certainly mentally disturbed by that enforced isolation and would usually perform a frantic rain dance when he saw us approaching. Dara would wag his tail in approval at the display, to our great amusement.

Once the fishing got underway, he sat amidships, eyes forward, to mark any sign of a fish rising. Then he would go rigid on the set until we reached the spot. When a fish was hooked he would reverse position to watch it coming around the back of the boat. Once netted and landed he gave the fish a single proprietary lick and again took up his forward station.

Dara was a superb swimmer. On the way back to shore he would sit forward on a vacant seat with constant glances back until I gave the word 'swim'. Then he would spring full length forward and accompany the boat to shore. On one occasion, in competition with a water spaniel, he won a £20 wager over a distance of a hundred yards from boat to shore. We must admit that while the spaniel was certainly some performer in the water, he had little or no experience of launching from a boat – as we had rightly anticipated! Dara hit the water swimming.

Daniel O had particular affection for Dara. This was certainly reciprocated, as was proved when Daniel O was confined to bed at home in Killarney. I had called to see him, leaving Dara out in the yard. When I came back to the car the dog refused to move until he was allowed up to see his friend. During that *turas báis* to Macernane, Dara never left Daniel O's side. When Daniel O staggered and fell on the kitchen floor, Dara came out in panic to alert me to the emergency. He was an amazing dog. With his death at the age of eighteen, carrying all those memories with him, he left a hole in my life. Fortunately, he left me son and daughter, Déise and Córa. Daniel O enjoyed the story of how Córa returned alone from their morning run making short dashes back in her evident excitement to bring me to accompany her. I found that they had a cat up a tree. Córa had left Déise to ride shotgun while she came for me to get it down. For that show of intelligence Dara was given all the credit by Daniel O – it was kind father for them.

8. The Stories You Hear ⚲

Last week I was reminded of happy days on Lough Derg on the Shannon, where a group of anglers would converge for the mayfly fishing. An angling companion of yesteryear had joined me at the funeral of a mutual friend who had often been with us in the Minogue family hotel at Scariff, which the cohort of mayfly anglers would take over for the season. As we spoke, the years rolled back to the 1970s when the mayfly fishing would have been the highlight of the angling diary. Lough Derg would have led the other lakes with the news that 'the fly is up'. That would have an electrifying effect on otherwise sober individuals, who would now abandon both home and work as they set off pell-mell for the west.

My friend recalled the craic and banter as we anglers sat around at night regaling the company with the mixed fortunes, mostly misfortunes, of the day. Faces blazing red from sun and wind. Eyes bloodshot from the glare off the dappled water. In those days factor 15 was not on the market. Undoubtedly, access to the bar helped to heighten the colour. The odd burst of laughter at some well-aimed sally added to the atmosphere.

It was amazing how total recall of stories rolled back the memory over thirty years or more. The group had little interest in the typical 'as-I-roved-out' fishing yarns. Those were dismissed as a tiresome waste of time. While one might varnish the truth to suit the company, a good story passed muster only if it had evidence and substance to it.

What gained applause was 'the music of what happened', the phrase used by Oisin to St Patrick in describing the doings of Fionn and the Fianna.

The story that was given pride of place was where three different animals had succeeded in landing three species of fish here in Ireland. Chapter and verse were supplied for each of the three incidents. It was a puzzle and so amazing in actual detail that there was no need to varnish it. A cat caught a trout, a dog a salmon, a calf a pike.

The trout had held its station for years under Ann Bridge near Maynooth. Nothing could entice a move from that safe haven where he patrolled his territory. It was impossible to get a fly to him. A shrewd angler retrieved a dead cat off the road, suspended it from the bridge and in time the blue-bottles provided a ready supply of maggots. As a maggot would plop into the pool, the fish would back down and lazily open its mouth. A hook baited with a maggot or two made history of that particular trout. I saw the actual fish displayed on his kitchen table by the proud angler. It was a beauty, all of three pounds. Nothing was lost in the telling of the exploit. 'He just made one mistake,' said the angler, 'Cunning as he was, if he had used a metal detector he would still be alive today!'

Now for the dog and the salmon. At low water, salmon would find it difficult to surmount the weir on the Mulcair, north of Limerick. A local had trained his German shep-herd to lay in wait for any fish struggling on the lip of the weir. Eventually patience would pay off and the dog would deliver the prize to his master, lurking in cover nearby. When charged with poaching, the human agent got off with the Probation Act and a caution. It would have given more colour to the story if the dog's owner had argued that he was unable to provide a salmon licence for the animal!

Finally, the calf and the pike. This incident was recorded from the Blackwater near Lismore. A farmer, on checking his stock, noticed that one calf had a mangled bloody nose. As he looked around he saw the body of a large pike on the grass beside the river. It was a fair conclusion that the pike, having grabbed the calf as it came down to drink, had then been stranded by the backward plunge of the panic-stricken animal.

As stories go, that was the winner. Still, on the Blackwater there were two further stories. The first proved the value of lateral thinking. An angler had hooked a salmon which ran the reel right out of line up the river. He looked sadly at the empty spool. He now realised that a hundred yards of nylon line was out there hanging in the current. Perhaps he could grapple it with a treble hook linked to a spare spool. All set for the contingency plan, he quickly got to work. Having succeeded in linking up the lines he began to reel in the salmon. His self-congratulation came to a sudden halt as he realised that he was now in the process of winding up two full lengths of line on to a single spool. Would he be lucky a second time? He allowed the salmon to rest as he sought out the original empty spool, transferred it to the reel and wound in the fish.

A further incident has been passed down in folklore about how a poacher succeeded in catching salmon on the opening day at the Duke of Devonshire's Careysville stretch of the Blackwater. He had laid a wager in a local hostelry that not only would he fish the stretch, but would succeed in obtaining the permission of the newly appointed water-keeper. The latter had come with a tough reputation for attention to duty. Our poacher was on the bank in good time on that first morning. As the water-keeper emerged from the house to have everything ready for his clients, he turned the air blue with some choice language when he saw someone already on the bank of the most favoured run. Straight into his vehicle and down hell-for-leather to accost the trespasser. He ordered the offender, in no uncertain terms about the charges pending for this blatant trespass, to reel up his tackle. Up came a meat hook baited with a spud! The poacher played the idiot. He explained that some men in the pub had told him that salmon eat spuds.

With a glint in his eye the water-keeper said: 'Fish away, my good man, you're quite right'. He could not wait to bring down his clients to share the experience. As he returned with his guest anglers his jaw dropped as he saw two salmon on the bank. 'You didn't catch those with the potato?' he said. 'Ah no, sir,' was the reply, 'I caught you with that!'

That friend whom I had met at the funeral surely made my day in that recall of stories. That night I prayed for all the companions who had enjoyed the simple pleasures of life on lake and stream. What strikes me now is the contrast between the leisurely pace of life in those times and the rush and stress of today's world.

Anglers are a strange bunch. In that family hotel in Scariff class or status did not count. The High Court judge and the leading consultant were cut down to size where necessary. What told was skill in the boat and humour at the table. Boasting of one's achievements attracted a chilling silence. There would be tolerance for short accounts of the ones that got away. 'Ah sure, they'll be still there for tomorrow'. Any 'shaggy dog' story got short shrift. The chorus of yawns spoke louder than the groans. It is difficult to fake attention when bed beckons after a day on the lake.

That little hotel in Scariff was truly an oasis. The company is engraved in my memory, which still reflects their characters as if it were yesterday. Indeed, however good the mayfly fishing at the time was it has paled before the recall of those evenings around the dinner table. That is still the focus of so many angling stories in my memory. I have since had a few experiences which would have been grist to the mill at that time.

One such experience did give great delight to an appreciative audience, which had been at the time observers of the action. If one had a video camera on site, the result would have qualified as a comedy of errors to beat anything seen on the Wild West rodeo circuit. I would rather not identify the star of the show, even though he now laughs uproariously when I remind him of the incident.

I have spoken already of Jim O'Callaghan, who had leased the salmon beats on the Shannon at Castleconnell outside Limerick. He had asked me to introduce a business partner to the ways of fishing for salmon when I was next passing through Limerick on my way home. For Beat 5 the casting distance requires a fourteen-foot, two-handed fishing rod. Getting one's back into it, one will have a lot of line in the air before shooting the final cast out over more than twenty yards of water.

My partner had the choicest of split cane rods and had spent hours practising his distance casting on the lawn at home. He was happy that he had found the rhythm and was now ready to display his skills. He appreciated my approval as he was left to his own devices. I was busy setting up my rod when I heard the commotion up the riverbank. What a sight! My friend was in full flight after a bullock into whose hide he had stuck the fly on the back cast. The rod was bent almost double as I shouted to him to stretch it out straight and let the bullock take the Hairy Mary. Else he would have made matchwood out of fourteen feet of choicest split cane.

A third party's shouted instructions on how to play the bullock were less than helpful.

The Mulcair weir features in many stories because the bridge which spans the river at that point was a grandstand for passing travellers who would often break the journey to watch the action when the salmon were running. The pool under the weir would always have a good supply of very excitable fresh run grilse. Naturally, this was where the anglers would congregate.

On one occasion, two reels on opposing banks began to run simultaneously. Both anglers had been fishing worm bait. It now dawned on them that they were playing the same fish! What had evidently occurred was that the salmon first hooked had crossed the other line. This would have left the angling see-sawing across the pool. An honest broker on the bridge resolved the situation by an offer to buy the fish and divide the price between the two anglers. Solomon could not have done better to sort out the predicament before the actors in the scene came to blows.

One of the biggest salmon ever caught on the Mulcair is said to have weighed in at over forty pounds on a coal scuttle scales at a shop in Castleconnell. I tell the story as I heard it from a witness.

A man on the way home from the local creamery stopped at the bridge to check the river. There he saw this huge fish attempting to negotiate the weir. Finally, it succeeded in the effort. The man with poaching experience surmised that the tired fish would rest at the first lie above the weir. From under the setlock of the cart he took his gaff with its wooden handle and length of rope attached. Moving up the river he saw the tired fish stationary under the bank as he had forecast. He made no mistake with the gaff. Then the action began.

Even with his experience he did not sufficiently allow for the power of the first mad plunge of that mighty fish. Pulled into the pool, he was forced to release the rope and drop down the current on to the weir. As he was getting his breath back he observed the rope surfacing and backing down towards the weir. As it got within reach he braced himself and hauled the now weakened fish on to the weir. There the story is as I heard it, albeit at second hand, but on trustworthy evidence.

One needs time in hand if you settle in to listen to the fortunes and misfortunes of old-time anglers. Never admit that you have heard the tale before because this can switch the storyteller off and leave him dead in the water, just as he was working around to his *pièce de résistance*. Never say 'yes' when you are asked: 'Have you heard this one?' It may be all in the telling and so should be given a hearing.

Have you heard the one about the goat that took the Blue Devon on the Feale and was reeled in by the angler who could not afford the loss of the bait? Have you heard the one about hooking the bat on the Pool at Ramelton and losing the cast of flies in a whitethorn bush? Have you heard the one about the salmon angler lighting a cigarette on the bridge at Banteer after a blank day and having a fish rise and take the butt? So the stories go.

That cigarette reminds me of a friend who had settled in to play a salmon well hooked on worm bait at Listowel. I had been standing by with net at the ready. Everything was now under control with the angler lighting up a cigarette to crown the satisfaction. On lifting back the rod to put more pressure on the fish he allowed the nylon line to come into contact with the cigarette tip. Calamity! He shook his head in disbelief and then reached for the cigarette box to discard it after the fish with a few blue maledictions. He did try hard but was unable to beat the addiction, in spite of that unhappy experience.

It is well known that fishermen are quite superstitious. This is particularly true of those who go to sea. I have heard a TV discussion which featured many such stories from the north Dublin coast. Certain animals were seen as star-crossed and unlucky. One did not dare use their proper names! The cat was called the long-tailed fellow, the rabbit the furry fellow and so on. I suppose that on going to sea one is taking one's life in one's hands, and so one is more than sensitive in regard to anything that might tip the balance.

I have known angler friends who follow a very set routine on the way to launching. One pattern which has a long history in folklore is always using the right leg first to step into the boat. This reflects the ancient belief that the left side is unlucky. The Latin term for left is *sinister*. It all reaches back, I believe, to sun worship. Going with the sun is turning right. Going against the sun is turning left. Therefore you should always begin a journey by putting the right foot forward. I have been told that a new trawler on being first taken to sea will turn right on leaving the harbour. I could add a long list of eccentric mannerisms and conditioned reflexes on which anglers depend to tip the scales in their favour. Once while sharing a boat with an ancient mariner he made a comment which I still treasure. It was one of those days when almost everything that could go wrong does. Forget the poor fishing, in that one always takes one's chances. What counted on this particular day were the happenstance disasters, ending with having to beach the boat to replace a broken shear pin on the propeller shaft of the outboard. As I produced the tools he shook his head and pronounced: 'You know what, Father, someone has turned the stones agin us this day!'

I could hardly believe my ears! Here was a comment I had never heard spoken in my life, even though I knew the background from what I had read about the ancient custom of 'turning the stones'. One turned them to the right to bless someone or something and to the left to bring a curse. It was common practice at sites in ancient times in Ireland where three or more round rocks were placed on a flat stone surface. One can see the site still at the Caiseal under Dá Cíoch Danann, south of Rathmore in Kerry. It is said that a British lady travelled to an island site in County Clare during World War II to turn the stones against Hitler!

Anyway, that comment of my companion on a day of disasters came back to me when I went with Dermot Linehan and Donal Creedon for my very first angling outing to Lough Caragh. The early warning came before we even got to the lakeside. Here we were driving along under the dappled shade of the trees when a dark shape materialised from the shadows right in front of us. As the car ground to a halt, the windscreen framed the horned head of a large black bull glaring at us.

I congratulated Dermot on his timely warning shout and proceeded to the lake. Everything looked grand as we boarded the boat and struck out along the mile-long channel to the fishing ground. As the water pump failed, the engine began to overheat and that was that. We rowed back thankful that it had not occurred away out the lake. With replacement engine running sweetly, we hove to and began a first drift over an area where brown trout, sea trout and grilse could be expected. Then it happened. Full of anticipation, Dermot shot out his line sharply to remove the memory kinks when, from his wet hand, off went rod and reel as well. New rod, new reel, new line – first day out! What made it more tragic was that they amounted to a very special combined birthday present to him from three of his angler sons.

That took away any further interest we had in fishing Lough Caragh. Would anyone blame us for believing that someone had turned the stones against us!

Now for a final story, one which I am happy to be around to narrate. We all wonder what thoughts would pass through our minds as we hover on the threshold of death. I will give you my reflections for what they are worth. What amazes me is the tranquility with which I left myself in God's hands. Similarly for my companion in peril.

It was the final day of the fishing season in Waterville and blowing hard. Earlier in the year this would not have been a day for the lake. But the last day? My companion Daniel O, whose expertise on boat matters always won any debate, proposed that we launch on Lough-na-Móna, one of the smaller upper lakes. Our trusted Johnson 6 engine got us safely across to the sheltered side. Within a short time the wind became really nasty and turned the lake into a maelstrom. As we were considering the option of beaching the boat and fishing the shore around to the car, the decision was taken out of our hands. A whirlwind tossed the boat over and decanted us upside down without more ado.

We well realised that the only hope in these circumstances was to get a grip on the boat and hold on for dear life as we assessed the options. Daniel O had been catapulted into the water in free fall, but fortunately I had held on to the gunnel. I reached down and grabbed him by the hair, of which he had always a fine mane on the back of his head. We locked our arms over the two seats and divested ourselves of the Wellingtons. There was no panic as we assessed our situation, hanging in that eerie green light under the boat.

In that position we felt that we were going nowhere

except around in a circle and that the cold would eventually seal our doom. It was agreed that I would drop outside, pull down on the keel enough to open the boat to the wind which would serve to turn it rightside up. The manoeuvre worked as planned and we were now in more command of the situation. All about us the lake was literally going up in smoke. However, waterlogged as the boat was with every wave washing over it and us, we could now make an effort to direct it towards shore as we hung on opposite sides in the water. What a blessed relief as we neared the shore when on stretching down a leg full length I encountered gravel!

That account foreshortens the hour and a half that we spent in the water. We crawled up the spit of sand on which the boat had beached and sat down to recover some energy. It was then that Daniel O asked what I had done with the flask of the home-brewed Kerry cordial. When I produced it from a pocket in my fishing jacket I earned no gratitude. On the contrary, with a twinkle in his eye, he claimed that my oversight in not producing it when really needed had almost cost him his life. He was then well into his seventies.

I am still amazed at how tranquil we were. Perhaps the fact that we were planning positively avoided the panic of a sense of hopelessness – even though we were certainly in mortal danger. We were in the hands of God and our prayers accepted that simple fact. Daniel O said that it was Confession time for him. He showed his appreciation with a smile when I remarked that we were not reduced to that yet! When matters became terminal I would be there for him – and then would need to take my chances with the mercy of God.

Another concern was to get around to warn two colleagues on the neighbouring Cloonaughlin Lake to make it ashore as the weather worsened. They did not believe our story until they saw us in our stockinged feet. Staying with the boat is essential even when waterlogged to the gunnels. After that experience we purchased lifejackets. Better not tempt Providence a second time.

9. The Coarse Fish Enthusiast ⌒⤙

Among traditional Irish game anglers, salmon and trout are what really count as fish worthy of the name on river or lake. The very term 'coarse fish' relegates all those species to a lower class both for sport and food. In Dallow and Allow, where I first cast a line on water, there were none of those coarse fish anyway. Indeed, to my knowledge of Irish angling of earlier times, angling for coarse fish simply did not register.

It was only when I came to read Izaak Walton's *The Compleat Angler*, written in England in the mid-1600s, that I came to appreciate how important angling for coarse fish was in Britain at that time. Having dealt with trout and salmon at some length, he devoted a dozen chapters to pike, carp, chub, grayling, bream, tench, perch, barbell, bleak, roach, ruffe and dace. Most of these I had barely heard about and certainly never encountered, except some pike, perch and dace as by-catch when fishing for trout and salmon. Indeed, many of those fish listed by Walton did not even exist here.

In Ireland today, angling for coarse fish in lakes and sluggish canals attracts even more enthusiasts than game fishing for salmon and trout. It is a major contributor to our tourist business and it runs right through the year. International festivals draw large numbers of big-spending competitors. If one looks through the bookshelves in sports emporia, one would notice that interest in coarse fishing is to the fore of game fishing. It certainly attracts many more young anglers. Perhaps the reason for this is the marked decline in salmon and sea trout stocks. We of an older generation are still sustained by the memory of glorious days in times past. Very few of us transfer our attentions late in life to coarse fishing. We continue to look with pity on anglers seated on their tripods on the bank of a canal with fishing poles stretched out over dead water. Their only activity seems confined to pitching out at intervals fistfuls of evil-smelling ground bait to keep fish in the vicinity. To us, this pastime qualifies as a parable for boredom – and the fish when caught are not even edible! Those same anglers go into a frenzy when they land what in their book counts as a specimen! A friend concluded that their only saving grace is that they do not clutter our waters.

Dace had become shining in their silvery scale coating, a plague in the Blackwater. They grab at our wet flies greedily and spoil one's expectations in many a promising trout ripple. It is reported that these intruders were given access to the Blackwater by pure chance when a box of live bait, brought across by a party of English coarse fishermen, had split open on the weir at Fermoy, having broken its mooring rope in a flood. That is just one example of how alien species have been introduced here. All too often, visiting anglers would discard leftover bait into lake or river at the end of their fishing holiday. Bringing any form of live bait into Ireland now attracts penalties. But it is too late for most, if not all, of our waters.

In a typical network of rivers and lakes, fish introduced at one spot will soon spread throughout the whole system. The Shannon is a good example. In addition, we have our waterbirds, which can transfer spawn from one feeding ground to another. Incidentally, this possibility has put paid to the anecdote that, given time, fish will self-generate. The anecdote owed its origin to the fact that coarse fish could appear in waters where they had not been introduced by human agency.

On Walton's list, one species should indeed qualify in their own right as game fish. The pike, and its legends, stands apart from others in the league. It is long-lived and grows to great size, registering up to half a hundred weight in Irish and English waters, and even more in Europe. Walton tells that a pike taken in Sweden in 1449 had a ring about its neck, which recorded in Greek that it had been released by Emperor Frederick the Second two hundred years before! One surely wonders whether there was a trickster at work.

When huge pike have been basking on the surface of Scandinavian lakes they may be dived on by fish eagles. I assume that these birds would be members of the white-tailed eagle species such as those mighty birds released in Killarney a few years ago. The osprey would hardly be large enough, even though one of these birds did take a ten-pound salmon from the Moy fishery at Ballina. To return to that Scandanavian report, eagles and hawks have talons that automatically lock on when they strike their quarry.

It is said that when attacked from the sky, a large pike would sound in a sudden dive and carry the unfortunate bird down with it. Later, the skeleton of the eagle may remain attached to the back of the fish and surface when the pike moves over the water. Hence the stories about fishermen scared out of their wits on seeing such a spectre approaching out of the mist. There it is as I heard it. Perhaps a too liberal recourse to the vodka or the schnapps on a cold winter evening may lie behind the story!

Pike were brought to Ireland, so it is said, by the Normans. It is certainly agreed that they are not native here. Therefore, in many parts of the country they are not found, simply because they have not been introduced. This is so in Kerry. In the Feale, in the Killarney and Waterville lakes and in the rivers that flow from them, pike are not to be found. That is surely a welcome omission. Pike are voracious in their feeding habits. Salmon and large trout frequently fall victim. The pike is the freshwater wolf, and once it sinks its savage set of backward slanting teeth into its target, with a sudden charge from its lair, there is no escape. The pike swallows its prize head-first, a practice which may seal the pike's doom if the meal jams in its throat. This has been frequently observed when a dead pike is later stranded on the shore with the evidence of its death still in place.

The pike is not selective in its feeding patterns. It will cruise along a reed bed and pull down any duck, coot, or waterhen that swims above. My aunt, who lived beside the Blackwater, often saw her clutch of ducklings or goslings devoured by pike. It is not unknown for a dog swimming in a lake or river to be pulled down. The sudden charge of the pike as it plucks a victim off the shallows reminds one of the crocodile. No wonder fearsome tales are told about them.

On a number of occasions, when fishing for salmon on the Blackwater, I have caught pike. Most of these would be small in size and known as jacks. Again, the typical charge at the bait would straightaway identify what fish it was. After one fast dash away it would give itself up. There would be nothing like the action one expects from a salmon or trout when hooked.

I never caught pike in the midland lakes, even though there were plenty of them in Ennell and Sheelin. They were usually caught on baits trolled for trout. The Inland Fisheries Trust aimed to limit their numbers in order to preserve the trout from their depredation by netting them on a large scale when they came inshore to spawn. Amazingly, the captured fish were then discarded because there was not a market for pike in Ireland at the time. In many parts of the Continent, the flesh is prized above that of salmon. Since then, pike fishing right through winter is a major attraction for big-spending angling tourists, who have recognised the potential in our lakes, canals and slow-flowing rivers. Formerly these tourists would have returned home with refrigerated vans stuffed with pike. However, there is now a strict limit on how many pike one may keep. All the rest must be released back into the water.

In former days, before recent measures of control, coarse fish, including pike, were there for the taking. A common practice was to fasten a bait fish such as a roach or perch to a bottle. This was then dropped into a lake for the wind to move it across as it bobbed on the wave. When the pike seized the bait he pulled the bottle under water. Eventually the constant fight against the upward pressure of the bottle would get the better of him. Come morning it would be found stranded on the windward shore. True, it was not a very sporting practice, but by all accounts it was quite effective.

Far more colourful a sport was that practiced on Lough Carra during certain hard winter frosts. Carra, near Ballinrobe, is an ideal location, with its shallow crystal-clear limestone water over a white marl bottom. It is one of the best waters in Ireland for large lake trout, particularly celebrated during the mayfly season. It holds a large number of pike as well.

When the lake is frozen solid enough to walk on with safety and with the ice cover clear of any coating of snow, sleet or hailstone, all is ready for the pike hunt. Through the transparent ice the target is located. The group of hunters closes in and tracks the fish as it moves from place to place. Eventually the pike tires from the action and settles on the bottom. Then a two-pronged hay fork is called into action. One prong is set on the surface of the ice and the other is spun to cut out a circular hole through which a gaff is lowered to haul up the fish.

It was a rare occasion when the conditions were just right, particularly the glass-like transparency of the ice cover. With so little frost in recent decades, the sport, if it should be so called, is a memory of the older generation. Another casualty of global warming! The press photographs at the time gave a truly amazing picture of groups of adults and children careering around the ice-imprisoned lake. They would be shod with heavy woolen stockings over the boots to give purchase on the ice. Once the accounts and pictures had been so published the pressure mounted to ban the practice. That left us with a contradiction. While the country people in the Carra area were forbidden to indulge in their traditional custom, the Inland Fisheries Trust continued under licence with a cull of pike as heretofore.

That Carra practice seems to have been the one form of physical exercise which was the exception to the typical sedentary pattern of coarse fish angling. When I was in Maynooth I frequently dropped along to competitions held on the Grand and Royal canals. The ritual was strict. The locations would have been staked out in advance and one took one's chances in the lottery for places. The amount of paraphernalia was impressive. At the core of the operation was the holding net, which contained the total catch, great and small, all mixed in together. Weight, not quality, was what counted at the weigh-in. Once the figure had been noted in the official results register, the fish were released back into the water.

Preservation of stock was a major concern. When immigrants from eastern Europe discovered the abundance of coarse fish in the Irish midland canals, it was a bonanza. For them, coarse fish is highly acceptable as an article of their ordinary diet. Most of us do not realise how substantial a dish a three-pounder bream provides for a family lunch. Naturally, there is tension between anglers who fish for the table and enthusiasts who return their catch to preserve stocks. There is need for some controls to assist good relations. An obvious measure of control would be a ban on net fishing and taking smaller fish.

Finally, we must not ignore how access to coarse fishing in Dublin and in other towns is such a boon for young anglers, who are so often deprived of healthy pastimes. Local authorities in many areas now stock fish, chiefly roach and perch, in local waters, to which the young have ready access. This is surely admirable and worthy of everyone's support. It is just hypocritical to continue to blame the young for the mayhem in which they too often engage when we do not provide attractive options for recreation. There are few better options than fishing, once young anglers are engaged at an early age. So let us end on that positive note in praise of coarse fish.

10. Perspective for the Future

On the Waterville front, any future for the sea trout fishery is parlous should the current situation continue. Right through the system from Lough Currane to the upper lakes, anglers now have had little or nothing to report after any amount of time spent on the water. It has arrived at the stage when one is surprised to see more than a single boat fishing for sea trout on any lake – and that same boat will call it a day after a few hours. Naturally there are some good luck stories, but these continue to be greeted with disbelief. The array of boats pulled high up on the shore at the various access points tells the true story. The collapse of the fishery has led to very few angling visitors, who were traditionally the bread and butter of tourism in Waterville. This downfall amounts to a very serious financial loss for gillies and for all those engaged in any area of the hospitality business. Early in the year, salmon anglers still come to try their luck as in times past. This indeed is welcome. To preserve the salmon stock the individual catch is severely restricted, a requirement which is generally accepted as a necessary measure for sustainability into the future.

Fishing for salmon too early in the season is not an acceptable option for conscientious anglers. They are unhappy about the number of spawned fish on their way to mend in the sea that are caught on the baits being trolled. Anglers may hook numerous emaciated fish in the process of landing a single fresh run salmon. This by-catch is terrible waste, particularly when sustainability is a very serious concern indeed. It beggars explanation why anglers universally do not move to delay the opening of the season for a month until late February. March 1 would seem a good option for D-day. By then all the salmon and sea trout kelts will have cleared the system. Another measure which should be required for the early days of the season is the use of a single hook rather than the current treble on the baits. This is the practice in New Zealand and does not mutilate the fish that are released.

Those who have fished over many years for sea trout in Waterville are in a position to contrast then and now. In former times, in the calm of the evening the lake surfaces would be pitted with sea trout on the move. Now the surface remains mirror still right through until darkness. In the past, knowledgeable anglers would launch their boats in late evening to fish the shallows where the sea trout would move in under cover of darkness to grub among the stones on the shore. If there are no fish on the feed, what is the point of launching a boat?

When I think of those glorious summer evenings on Lough Currane nostalgia puts a lump in the throat. In the words of W.B. Yeats, evening there would be a 'purple glow'. This is the glory of the west of Ireland as the summer sun drops below the horizon and reflects off the Atlantic in an hour-long twilight. This is where the people of the Holy Land got their proverb, even though the Mediterranean would not have the reflecting extent of our Atlantic Ocean. Jesus remarked: 'It will be fair weather; for the sky is red'. (Matthew 16:2) We in Ireland have our version: 'A red sky at night, the shepherd's delight, a red sky in the morning, the shepherd's warning'.

As one pushed out the boat on those summer evenings one's heart would rise in gratitude to the Creator. An old companion of mine would have pronounced the Gaelic benediction: *'Buiochas mór le Dia na cruinne'.* For us the time to be on the lake would have been just before sundown when the sand martins came down to feed on the flies off the lake. The flock would arrive like clockwork to circle over their favourite feeding grounds and dip on to the surface where the flies were hatching. If one did not meet fish on the move at that witching hour, one would wait until darkness to try your luck on the shore shallows.

In days past, as the time for spawning in November arrived, one would check the areas of gravel at inlet and outlet bays of the various lakes. There the fish would be milling around competing for space to excavate redds in which to deposit the eggs. Lough-na-hEisge in front of the house at Macernane was a favourite location. We would visit those gravel areas in anticipation of counting on a healthy future for the sea trout stock. Comparisons would, of course, be drawn with former years.

There cannot be a better estimate of the health of the future run of sea trout than the evidence for all to see on those gravel beds. The gravel apron at the outlet of Lough-na-hEisge had been built up in the early 1990s by Seán O'Leary and myself from the extensive gravel deposits at the foot of the ravine at Bun-na-hEisge. I have referred to this already. This was the ideal solution for restoring spawning grounds because one is using the type of gravel material from the actual locality. On a calm lake, running the boat up and down was no effort. We took turns at the work – one filling the bags while the other ran the boat down to deliver the gravel. It was a labour of love. Lough-na-hEisge, which since then had been closed to fishing for a number of years precisely to preserve the future stock, was the ideal testing ground. The spawning story now is almost at standstill after the gradual decline of recent years.

As is the case with any threat to a natural resource, once the symptoms are clear, the aim will be to discover the causative factors. Of course, if there is a sudden collapse in the resource that search should be quite straightforward. Matters are more difficult with a gradual decline, which may indicate a combination of factors.

The introduction of salmon farming in estuaries, which were the typical feeding grounds of sea trout, attracted blame almost immediately. The evidence was there in the multiplication of parasitic sea lice, which came to infest the sea trout. Then, in order to control these parasites and other contagions and infections which arise where great numbers of salmon are crowded together in confined spaces, chemicals would have been sprayed over the holding cages. These chemicals in turn dropped to the sea floor and combined there with the food debris, which the sea trout would then consume. That would amount to a toxic cocktail, which certainly would affect fish which are highly sensitive to pollution of any kind.

That term 'pollution' also rings a death knell for sea trout in inland waters where the catchment area and its feeder streams may be subject to run-off from sewage systems, industrial waste and intensive farming. The media keep us informed on the many fish kills so arising. With so many flat catchment areas inland, the flow in our rivers is sluggish in flushing out pollutants. However, the Waterville network of lakes and rivers has its sources in hilly terrain and neither is it subject to those forms of pollution just mentioned. There is little doubt that the siting of a large commercial mink farm on the lakeshore at Lough Currane was ill-considered, to put it very mildly. That certainly was a source of pollution in early years but that problem now seems to have been substantially rectified.

We must now turn attention to the widescale netting at sea as a commercial industry. This principally affected salmon on their migratory return to their parent rivers on the way to spawn. The larger sea trout which had accompanied them to their northern feeding grounds were now returning in their company. The major salmon run back to Irish rivers swings around Bloody Foreland in Donegal, then right down our west coast to skirt south and east. On this migratory return run the fish travel at quite a shallow depth where nets can readily reach down to them.

In days gone by, the coarse cord nets then in use were visible and so would be avoided by the fish, except on dark moonless nights. Today's monofilament gill nets are invisible and highly efficient at taking fish in all weather conditions. They stretch out for miles on end and take everything that comes that way, including dolphins and diver birds. If left unattended for longer periods, predatory seals do major damage to the trapped fish. Then should a net or a series of joined nets break loose from their moorings, they still continue to kill fish as they 'ghost' along in the sea currents.

Monofilament netting at sea is now to end in terms of a buy-out scheme put in place by the state, under pressure from other countries who already have stringent controls in place. If Greenland has preserved the salmon's feeding grounds we would surely be seen as greedy and unprincipled if we were to benefit by their restraint. So with the monofilament nets out of commission we await the good results, not just with salmon but with the larger sea trout for which Waterville was famed. Of course, there has always been a question about the numbers of wild sea trout on hotel and restaurant menus when very few were being caught legally. *Sinn ceist eile,* as we Irish would remark conspiratorially.

As the saying goes, 'Better light one candle than curse the darkness'. You must start somewhere. Here a company of gillies and some of us anglers fell to work to provide better access through the feeder streams and to improve the spawning beds. A lot of valuable work was done and in the process morale among all interested parties increased to replace the sense of gloom, which would have otherwise prevailed. Actually, it takes few enough spawning fish to keep the system healthy. Much depends on the adequacy of the food supply available to sustain the young fry as they grow into parr and smolts until they get safely to sea. This puts a query over the value of fish hatcheries, which release large numbers of smolts into waters poor in feeding, with competition from a resident population already in possession.

This brings me to my friend and colleague Michael Gass and to the efforts that he is making to get to the bottom of what happens to the sea trout when they return from the salt water into our lakes. He surely knows the business after a lifetime's experience of fishing in Waterville. The only access for salmon and sea trout is through Butler's Pool at Waterville House, so that the fish counter there should provide a fair record of what comes in, if it registers accurately. The figures reported seem healthy enough. That then begs the questions: 'Where do those fish go? What happens to them?'

It was Michael Gass who pointed out that the water in Cloonaughlin, the lake with which we are most familiar, had turned gin clear in contrast to its former more typical cloudiness. What had happened to the algae and other microscopic entities that should have been in suspension as a crucial layer in the food chain? If that food chain is compromised the quality of the whole habitat is in crisis. That set him thinking about a likely reason for this change. After some detective work, he considered that the increased exposure to ultraviolet rays may have had some such clarifying effect on the water. That might also explain why the fish were not to be found in the upper layers where they would rise to the lures that anglers presented. In gin-clear, transparent water they might not feel comfortable and so would seek the depths for security, until the drive to spawn got them moving late in the season when they are quite out of condition. Should we look to the thinning ozone layer as the reason why ultraviolet rays now penetrate the atmosphere to a greater degree than formerly and drive the fish down?

Whatever about the sea trout, even more inexplicable was the absence of brown trout in any shape or form in lakes where they had been abundant until quite recent times. Indeed, when fishing for sea trout, an angler would have avoided certain areas where the small brownies were a distraction as they grabbed at the flies as soon as the line hit the water. Even in those areas the little fellows were absent. In places where the inflow of a stream in flood might have muddied the lake water, a few trout might be encountered – just a few. It all amounted to a puzzling scenario.

Michael Gass decided to proceed further with his enquiries. At his own expense, in the summer of 1996 he brought an expert from Scotland to conduct a survey of the lakes to discover the actual fish population. It involved a most interesting series of experiments. The method employed was to set what are known as tangle nets at various depths and await results overnight. These nylon tangle nets are quite unusual, but the name indicates just what they are and how they work. They entangle everything great or small that wanders into them. Of course we were to learn that disentangling those tangle nets after use is a wearying task.

The following morning we were out on Cloonaughlin, all expectant. The results surprised us: very few sea trout, some more brown trout, but a large concentration of char. The latter ran to around five inches in length. We had not realised that they were so common because they rarely enough take a fly and they come to spawn along the lake shore after the trout fishing season has ended. From the half consumed state of many of them it was evident that the eels favoured their oily flesh.

The survey of the other hill lakes proved little different in results. The char were everywhere in evidence at midwater in the deeper parts. We expected to find char in Lough-na-mBreac Dearg (*Breac Dearg* is the Irish for char) but they were widespread in the system. I was surprised to be told that our little fish were of the same species as the Arctic char, which grow very large on the rich feeding grounds in those cold waters.

We still await the full report on the survey but the evidence is clear enough. Whatever the reason, both sea trout and brown trout would appear to be in short supply in the upper lakes at Waterville. On the reason or the combination of reasons for that, the jury is still out. Michael Gass is now considering the value of taking silt cores from the lakes to identify what changes have occurred in the sediment layers, which might throw some light on what is currently taking place.

One spin-off from the tangle net survey in the upper lakes that had discovered the large population of char, is the likelihood that ferox trout are present. Char is their favourite prey and they grow large through feeding on that rich, oily food source. Ferox, on best evidence, is basically a lake-dwelling brown trout which has turned cannibal. When it comes to catching them they are selective and almost exclusively confine their interest to char. By exception they may take a large salmon lure on a trolling line. I have described already how Daniel O's good fortune in one morning on Killarney's Lough Lein left him with three salmon and three ferox trout. I saw the evidence in the boot of his car. Those trout were monsters indeed, every single one well over ten pounds and each larger than the salmon. Over the years, there have been reports from Killarney of outsize trout being taken by salmon anglers.

Naturally, when I observed those fish in the boot of Daniel O's car it put some of my own experiences in a new perspective. One June morning, following on a very welcome night of rain after a long drought, Fr John O'Keeffe and I went out on Lough-na-Móna. It was mirror calm, when quite close to us, on the deepest corner of the lake, we observed some very large fish lazily circling, barely breaking the surface with their dorsal fins as they coasted along. This was a unique sight in our experience. Thinking that they were salmon we tried large flies and we cast baits ahead of the fish. They ignored every lure we threw at them and in their own time submerged without a ripple on that calm lake.

I reported the experience to a gillie friend, to be told that very early in the season the few anglers trolling for salmon would have reported something similar in that same area of the lake. None of these fish ever bothered with any lure. Perhaps they were outsize sea trout but, if so, some should have been taken on salmon lures as they would have been early in the season on Lough Currane.

The mystery remained but it haunted me, as I hoped some day to make direct contact with one of these monsters. Perhaps I did, perhaps I didn't. Anyway, some years later, out on Cloonaughlin with my Donegal Capuchin friend Fr Mark Coyle, it was blowing a south-western near gale. As we crossed over to calmer water I had left the fly line to trail behind the boat. A small fish grabbed one of the flies and, as I reeled it in to release it, I sensed extra weight on the line. We were now in calmer water and as I took in more line I saw this large dark shadow following on. Whatever it was that little fish had been well chewed. Casting it out again behind the boat it was grabbed a second time.

This sure was crisis time for this pair of anglers. What to do? Let the monster carry on with his meal in the hope that he would swallow it hook, line and sinker? Subsequently, playing it to the boat on a light nylon cast would have been a miracle if it succeeded. Better get the bait rod ready with a treble hook attached to one of our smaller brown trout. The fish took his own decision and simply moved away, leaving the rest of his meal to us. What was it? Salmon, outsize sea trout – or ferox? If you wish to know what a fisherman's dreams are made of when the achievement of a lifetime evades him, refer to Ernest Hemingway's *The Old Man and the Sea.*

One must accept that the ferox is a most elusive fish, highly selective in his diet. He confines his menu almost exclusively to char, and there is no shortage of these. Many of the small catch that anglers discard in the course of a day are undoubtedly char. They are quite similar to brown trout in shape but the scales are somewhat smoother and their colour more ruddy. Their Irish name, *Breac Dearg,* reflects that. The ferox certainly knows the difference. The

Scotsman with the tangle nets is a specialist on fishing for ferox trout. We look forward to seeing him test the potential of Waterville.

I was heartened about the future of the sea trout when I read Major R.A. Chrystal's *Angling Theories and Methods*. It was written in 1927 when sea trout were plentiful in Scotland. Chrystal would seem to have been a full-time angler, not unusual at the time. He is well regarded. His conviction is that sea trout are no other than brown trout, which in search of better feeding have worked their way down into estuaries as slob trout and eventually out to sea. In the process they do not lose their drive to return to spawn in their native streams. This is what he says on p. 28:

> It is common knowledge that fresh water and sea trout spawn together and interbreed, yet no noticeable 'hybrids' have been observed. It is safe to assert that the evolution of sea trout is a continuous process, which is going on, year after year to this day, and that the stock can never die out as long as fresh water trout exist to reinforce it.

If the worst were to happen, then, in the shorter term anyway, it would be good to hope that our sea trout are not beyond the point of no return. Meanwhile, we might turn to the rainbow trout, known by the beautiful Latin name *Salmo Irideus*. These are native to the rivers of California and other states. When they return after migration to the sea these steelheads, as they are known, provide first-class game fishing.

Rainbow trout have been introduced into these islands for over a century and have been stocked into many land-locked lakes and worked-out quarries. They are fished for throughout the whole year and provide good sport when other game fish are out of season. That requirement for land-locked waters underlines the fact that, in our lands, rainbow trout will migrate to the sea and not return.

Any way out, no matter how unlikely, will be discovered and the rainbows disappear. I have fished for them on occasion and the angling requires special skills and lures. The main drawback is that the waters where they are stocked may be sited in very featureless areas. This environment would not make them, for me at any rate, an attractive option. The experience was not unlike that at a driven shoot with hand reared pheasants. It hardly qualifies as sport when a clay pigeon session is more acceptable.

A day out in the open country with a pair of red setters working rough terrain leaves you with memories – even though you may bring home little in the line of game. In fact, you would feel apologetic about shooting anything were it not to hearten the dogs. In this connection, the thought of fishing for rainbow trout in the glorious environment of Glenbower Wood near Killeagh in east Cork did promise a treat. My appetite had been honed by an evening on a stocked lake at Moll's Gap in the hills south of Killarney.

Well you guessed it! When I finally had plans made I found that those stocked rainbow in Glenbower had disappeared as if the lake had swallowed them. Where could they have gone with the only outlet barred with a grid? Was it possible that they had jumped the grating? Major Chrystal reports a similar experience with stocking rainbows into a grated mill dam. The dam pool was denuded of rainbows in a short time. Some of them were later caught down in the mill stream.

Perhaps we will need to look at the option of sea fishing. Here, south-west Kerry promises well on this front. The

Gulf Stream is within range of the shore. My neighbours, the Linehans, have taken up sea fishing to fill the gap left by the decline of sea trout. They bring home a variety of fish, everything you would find in a well-stocked fishmonger's shop. Bass are now in short supply because they are so slow growing. They really are the choice in shore angling and they should surely qualify as game fish.

To all this we must add the influence of global warming on the sea around the south-west. Fish from tropical waters are now moving further north. Anyone who has made the sea trip around Sydney harbour may have been rewarded with a sighting of a sunfish rolling along lazily, looking quite like a black Volkswagen Beetle. Well now you may see them, as I did, if you make the boat trip to the Skelligs from Valentia.

What has really caught the imagination has been the news of tuna being landed far out west from Dingle. These are serious game fish which normally run up to fifty kilos in weight and travel very fast in the ocean. On powerful sea tackle they give a good account of themselves. Again they are moving up to us from the Bay of Biscay. You can now add a codicil, some codicil this! What preys on the tuna is the swordfish, the focus of interest in Hemingway's *The Old Man and the Sea*. Now there's a thought. Dream on!

Afterglow ⌒⌒

The cover picture recalls the Black Bridge at Ballinatona as I knew it when I first came to fish the Dallow. The river then had a fine flow of limestone water from the Blessed Well a few hundred yards to the west. It was the limestone quality that produced the fine trout which attracted the local angling fraternity, fish of a pound or more. The river maintained a constant height from that permanent source and ran clear as gin over its gravel bed. It would raise the heart of any fly fisherman.

In a spate when the flood came tearing down from the extensive catchment area, it was a different river as it ran muddy and bank high. Then one appreciated why the arch of the bridge was so large and so sturdily built with blocks of the local Meelin limestone, which was in such demand for structures where weathering was the essential factor.

Today the Dallow at Ballinatona is a shadow of what it was fifty years ago. The pristine clear limestone flow is no more. It has been siphoned off to provide water for a number of towns and villages in the Duhallow regions. We are left with the surface water, which drains from the shale and sandstone of the area. At summer height the stream is little more than a trickle.

I want to recall the Dallow at Ballinatona as it really was. With that thought one man came to mind straightaway – David Willis, a Mallow neighbour and a fellow angler. He is known nationally as a superb painter from his television programmes on TG4. Recently the theme of one of these programmes was an exercise in painting the weir across the Dallow in the riverside park at Kanturk. I said immediately, 'That's the very man!' Having seen the fine structure of the Black Bridge and heard me speak about it in days gone, he has employed his gifts as an artist to envisage that scene as it was when my angling friends and I leaned over the parapet to assess what promise the day held.